The Smalbanac 2.0

The Smalbanac 2.0

An Opinionated Guide to New York's Capital District

Christine M. Garretson-Persans

excelsior editions

State University of New York Press
Albany, New York

Published by State University of New York Press, Albany

Printed in the United States of America

Excelsior Editions is an imprint of State University of New York Press

For information, contact State University of New York Press, Albany, NY
www.sunypress.edu

Production by Jenn Bennett
Marketing by Fran Keneston

Library of Congress Cataloging-in-Publication Data

Names: Garretson-Persans, Christine M., author.
Title: The Smalbanac 2.0 : an opinionated guide to New York's capital district / by Christine M. Garretson-Persans.
Description: Albany : State University of New York Press, 2016. | "Excelsior Editions." | Includes bibliographical references and index.
Identifiers: LCCN 2016031498 (print) | LCCN 2016043117 (ebook) | ISBN 9781438463605 (pbk. : alk. paper) | ISBN 9781438463629 (e-book)
Subjects: LCSH: Albany (N.Y.)—Guidebooks.
Classification: LCC F129.A33 G37 2016 (print) | LCC F129.A33 (ebook) | DDC 91.747/4304—dc23
LC record available at https://lccn.loc.gov/2016031498

10 9 8 7 6 5 4 3 2 1

Welcome to the updated and revised Smalbanac! We love the Capital District and want you to love it too, so we've put together a new Smalbany almanac with a pile of stuff that we really like about living here.

Inside you'll find more history! More drama! More things to do! More food, more shopping, and more of everything we like!

** A Note About Our Listings **

All of the phone numbers in the Smalbanac are in the 518 area code unless otherwise noted. We have listed only places we have visited, so if you are not in this edition, don't feel bad—there's always next time. We hope to publish an updated edition (like this one!) every few years, so if you have comments or suggestions, please visit us at www. smalbanac.com.

Contents

Albany—An Oldie but a Goodie

Albany is one of the oldest cities in America, depending on whose rules you use. Using the "longest continually chartered city" rule, Albany (officially chartered in 1686) is the oldest. It's been more than 400 years since Henry Hudson sailed up our river looking for a passageway to Asia. He never found one, but his voyage of 1609 was the beginning for Albany.

The first fur-trading fort, Fort Nassau, was built by the Dutch in 1614. (Special note: don't build forts on tiny islands in a tidal river.) Fort Orange was built on the western shore of the not-yet-named Hudson River in 1624, and was where the city would eventually rise. Fort Orange became Beverwijck or Beverwyck, and later Albany, when the British took over. It was named for the Duke of York and Albany, who became King James II. Fort Orange was used as a trading post for beaver pelts, and manned by settlers brought over by patroons in exchange for large tracts of land.

Killian Van Rensselaer was the first patroon, and in exchange for bringing 50 settlers to Fort Orange, he received about 800,000 acres of land on either side of the Hudson. Although he never set foot here, the Van Rensselaer name lived on. Even after the British took over in 1664, the patroon system was kept in place for another 200 years, until the last patroon, Stephen Van Rensselaer III, pretty much threw in the towel. He let the land leases lapse, and didn't go after rent due, leaving his son, Stephen IV (who inherited the title, land, and all the debts upon his father's death), with no way to collect past rents. The Anti-Rent War raged in and around Albany for seven years. Bye-bye patroonships.

With the looming French and Indian War, in 1754, representatives from seven of the colonies met at what was known as the Albany

Congress to discuss plans for a common defense against the French in Canada and how to improve relations with local Native Americans. Ben Franklin used the opportunity to present his Albany Plan of the Union, which was to unite the colonies under a common president selected by the Crown. The colonies were not quite ready to give up their individual powers for a central government, but it was this plan that was the model for the Stamp Act Congress, which was our dress rehearsal for the Declaration of Independence.

In 1797, Albany became the state capital. As well as being the seat of state government, with the politics that go with that, the city grew in stature as a place of manufacturing, shipping, and finance. The Erie and Champlain canal systems put Albany at the center of everything. It was the destination of the first steamboat, the "North River Steamboat" (Clermont). Not only were we famous for manufacturing the three B's— baseballs, billiards, and beer—but we were number one in the production of aspirin, potato chips, caps and gowns, spring beds, *and* toilet paper. After the Depression, most of that disappeared. Not the hot air, though.

Erastus Corning 2nd was mayor from 1941 until he died in 1983, and he was a firm believer in the status quo. Nothing changed for years and years. He wouldn't take any federal money for city improvements, so we stagnated for a little while. The upside of this is that we still have some of our historic buildings, including the beautiful Union Station.

When Nelson A. Rockefeller became governor, he talked Corning into the Empire State Plaza project. This of course wiped out the heart of Albany, replacing it with concrete. The construction of Interstate 787 completely cut the city off from the river that gave Albany its life. Rockefeller had vetoed the State Museum and the original convention center, but Corning fought to have these put back in the plans. Although much history was lost during this project, the city seemed to realize how important 400 years is in the scheme of things and started making real progress in preserving and celebrating the past. With the opening of the Hudson River Way overpass in 2002, you can walk to the river again and enjoy its beauty.

Albany is rising as a technological go-to destination, and small entrepreneurs are starting to make things here again—Beer! Alcohol! Even soap! There's great music, great food, spectacular parks, and a giant Nipper dog watching over us. Our city motto is "Assiduity," which means perseverance with a purpose. Four hundred years is a testament to that. Stop in to the Albany Visitors Center at Clinton Avenue and Broadway to get all the info you need to find what you want.

Hurlbut to Turkey—Getting from Here to There

Albany's landscape presented an unusual challenge to anyone who liked any kind of order. Bordered by the river to the east and hills to the west, with ravines here and there, and three large streams making their way through town to the river, the city had a natural geography that made planning an organized street map fairly problematic. Early on, the streets followed the land and its features, and the names were fairly self-explanatory. State Street was always the main street, sometimes called Yonker (young lord—a title of importance), and is still called State. What is now Broadway was Market Street, where there was a huge central market building and businesses lining either side. Court Street, where the old State House and court building were, is now an extension of Broadway. Grass and Cow Lanes led you down to the pastures from the city center. Barrack Street (now Chapel) was near the fort, Quay and Dock near the water. Watervliet Street led you north to you-guessed-where, and Middle Lane was somewhere in the middle.

In 1794, Simeon De Witt, a surveyor, was asked to map out a proposed street system for Albany. He planned two perfect grids, one west of Eagle Street and one in the pastures. The east-west streets in the central grid were to be named for mammals; from north to south, they were Hare, Fox, Elk, Lion, Deer, Tiger, Buffaloe, Wolf, Otter, and Mink. The north-south street were to be named for birds; going west from Eagle Street, they were Hawk, Swan, Dove, Lark, Swallow, Snipe, Duck, Pigeon, Turkey, Sparrow, and Partridge. By 1813, Evert Van Alen, the new surveyor for the city, mapped this same grid out, and as people began to populate the west side of the city, the new names were put in place. Fox ran along Foxes Creek, which later was buried in underground pipes. The street above was renamed Canal Street, and today it is Sheridan. Foxes Creek has been buried literally and figuratively.

Of all the mammals, only Elk survived. Elk had replaced Queen Street, as Lion had replaced King. Names were changed to honor presidents (Lion to Washington Avenue), to honor heroes (Northern Boulevard to Henry Johnson Boulevard), to mark achievements (Clinton Avenue to honor Governor Clinton, "father of the Erie Canal"), and sometimes just because someone didn't like it. Duck became Robin, Turkey became Quail, and Snipe became Lexington Avenue.

Which brings us to Hurlbut. What! Is it a verb? A noun? Actually, Elisha P. Hurlbut, who lived most of his life in the Albany area, finished his public life as a Supreme Court justice in New York. A staunch supporter of civil rights and equality for all people, and an opponent of the influence of organized religion in politics, he was way ahead of his time for the 1850s. Earlier in his career, in 1843, he made passionate arguments in favor of tenants in the local Anti-Rent War. His *Essays on Human Rights and Their Political Guaranties*, which he spent his last 30 years writing, is still available and may be worth rediscovering.

Places to Visit in Albany

Albany Board of Education: In Academy Park across from the capitol (the first Albany Academy). This is one of our buildings designed by Philip Hooker around 1813. Herman Melville attended the academy during his Albany days, pre-*Moby-Dick*. This is also where the great American scientist Joseph Henry performed his first experiments with electricity. It is surrounded by a conifer garden with more than 300 types of evergreens, and no, we didn't count them, but feel free. The Albany Beautification Committee installed a, yes, beautiful fountain in the northeast part of the park in 1988.

Albany City Hall: 24 Eagle Street, Albany, between Pine and Lodge. While the capitol was being built, the old city hall burned down. The stone carvers were in town, and H. H. Richardson, a lead architect working on the capitol, was chosen to design a new city hall. It is made of Rhode Island granite, and has some really outstanding design details. The outside was finished in a few years, but due to financial constraints, it took another 35 years to complete the interior. The building has a 49-bell carillon that is played at noon on Tuesdays and Wednesdays, and also on special occasions. City Hall houses the mayor's office, the Common Council chamber, and other city departments. A statue of Philip Schuyler is located in front of the building.

Albany Institute of History and Art: 125 Washington Avenue, Albany, 463-4478. This is one of the oldest art museums in America. It houses an eclectic collection of artifacts, paintings, furniture, and just stuff (including a mummy) that provide a very thoughtful glimpse into Albany's past. The institute has wonderful educational programs, and is very active with the City Neighbors Project. There is an admission fee, which is waived during Albany's First Friday from 5 to 8 p.m. If you are looking for a special gift, there is an outstanding gift shop on the second floor.

Albany Rural Cemetery: 48 Cemetery Avenue (off Broadway), Menands, 463-7017. When the old Dutch cemetery at the bottom of State Street started flooding on a frequent basis, it was decided that a new "rural" cemetery had to be built and the graves moved. This cemetery was incorporated in 1841 and formally dedicated in 1844. All of the churches in Albany had their own graveyards; however, by 1866 it was decided that all of the remains of old Albanians had to be moved out of town and into Albany Rural. This cemetery is really beautiful, and a great place to take a walk while learning a bit about the city's history. There are a lot of interesting people buried here, including Samuel O. "One-Armed" Berry (1839–1873), who was part of a gang of murderers and thieves that included James Younger and Frank James. He died in jail after serving seven years of hard labor for committing multiple murders. Others include Troy's Henry Burden of the Ironworks fame; C. E. Dudley, whose wife donated money to build the Dudley Observatory; Philip Hooker, the architect; all three Erastus Cornings; a Quackenbush; Herman Melville's father; Ten Eycks galore; Stephen Van Rensselaer III, the last patroon of Albany; a slew of Schuylers, including Philip (one of the family headstones is installed upside down so it takes longer to read); Elisha P. Hurlbut, New York Supreme Court judge and namesake of Hurlbut Street near the Spectrum; and of course Chester Alan Arthur, the 21st US president, who has one of the oddest looking angels caressing his grave with a palm frond. Look for the American flag, and you have found him.

Albany Heritage Area Visitors Center: 25 Quackenbush Square, Albany, 434-0405. Quackenbush Square is located at the corner of Clinton Avenue and Broadway in Albany. The Visitors Center is housed half in the old water department building and half in the old pumping station building. It has a great little museum that offers a quick history of Albany, and has a really good orientation film that provides an overview of the city. The Visitors Center also houses the Henry Hudson Planetarium, which offers shows the third Saturday of every month at

11 a.m. and 1 p.m. for only $3. If you can find it, it is open seven days a week and has a great staff to help you find your way into downtown.

Alfred E. Smith Building: South Swan Street, Albany. The Alfred E. Smith building was built between 1927 and 1930 and was named for a four-term governor who also had the misfortune to be the Democratic Party's nominee for president in 1928 (Herbert Hoover was the other guy). At 388 feet high, with 34 stories, it was the tallest building in Albany until the Corning Tower was built. During construction of the Smith building, if you looked at the site from the river (when we had a river that you could look up from), it looked as if the long-forgotten dome was being added to the state capitol building. Its four-year renovation was completed in 2006. Everything was spiffed up, including the lobby's ceiling mural of famous New Yorkers by noted local mural painter David Lithgow. The outside façade, with all 62 New York counties engraved in it, is really a nice touch for the first really big state office building. If you want to go inside it usually is open from 7 a.m. to 7 p.m. weekdays, and you can try to guess who's painted on the ceiling.

Anneke Janse Bogardus Plaque: No building, or statue, just a plaque on State Street in Albany, near James Street where her house once stood. The plaque reads, "Upon this corner stood the house occupied by and wherein died Anneke Janse Bogardus 1663." You've probably walked by this hundreds of times, and maybe you've wondered who Anneke was. She was born around 1605 in Amsterdam, married Roelof Jansen, and moved to Rensselaerwyck in 1630, making her one of the earliest settlers. Within five or six years, they moved to New Amsterdam (New York City), and Roelof was given 62 acres of so-so farmland smack in the middle of what would become Manhattan. They had six children. Roelof died in 1637, within a year of his sixth child's birth. In 1638, Anneke married the Rev. Everardus Bogardus, with whom she had another four children. After the reverend died at sea on a trip to visit Amsterdam in 1647, the widow Bogardus moved back to Fort Orange to be near her daughter. She died here around February 23, 1663, and was buried next to the Old Dutch Reformed Church at State and Broadway. Anneke's remains were moved to Albany Rural Cemetery by 1867. She left her 62 acres in Manhattan to her children, but somehow the land ended up in the hands of Trinity Church, and it has been in litigation since the 1700s with only the lawyers making any money. There are dozens of Anneke Janse and Everardus Bogardus descendant associations across America. She apparently has approximately a million heirs. Catharine Van Rensselaer Schuyler is one of them.

Empire State Plaza: 98 acres of concrete located between Madison Avenue and Swan, State, and Eagle streets, Albany. Corning was mayor; Rockefeller was governor. Rocky wanted a really cool legacy, so he moved out entire neighborhoods in order to knock down more than 1,000 buildings. Although he was governor, Rockefeller was called the best mayor Albany ever had for turning the city around. The plaza is home to the state museum (really fun and has a great changing art gallery), Corning Tower with a free observation deck on the 42nd floor (one floor for each year Corning was mayor), four other towers, the concourse with an extensive modern-art collection, the Vietnam Memorial, and of course the Egg, without which our skyline would not be nearly as distinctive.

First Church: 110 N. Pearl Street, Albany, 463-4449. This Dutch Reformed church was built in 1798 and was designed by Philip Hooker (who designed a lot of the nicer old buildings in town). Inside is the oldest pulpit in America, sent over in 1656 for the original First Church. This one has an hourglass on it to keep the sermons to an acceptable length. If your Sunday morning hangover keeps you from going inside, you can sit in the parking lot for the drive-in service all summer long. The rooster weathervane on top is an exact replica of the one that was brought over with the hourglass—complete with bullet holes. The original is inside, protected from the elements. If you love Louis Comfort Tiffany, First Church has an absolutely gorgeous Tiffany window inside by its offices. This was Teddy Roosevelt's church when he was governor, and his pew is marked with a plaque.

Fort Crailo: 9½ Riverside Avenue, Rensselaer, 463-8738. Fort Crailo was built in 1712 by Hendrick Van Rensselaer on the 1,500-acre estate that was part of his grandfather Kiliaen's original patroonship. It had a small fort on the property dating back to the 1600s, and was used for the quartering of troops during various wars. It was during the French and Indian War that a British surgeon, housed here alongside the colonists, wrote the song "Yankee Doodle" to make fun of the rather ragtag appearance of the locals. Hendrick's granddaughter Catharine Van Rensselaer, who eventually would marry Philip Schuyler, was raised here. There is an old ghost story about a Gertrude Van Twiller who was "borne away by Indians" while sitting by the river, and never heard from again—except for her screams in the night. The fort is open Wednesdays through Sundays, mid-May through the end of October, 11 a.m. to 5 p.m., with tours on the hour.

The Governor's Mansion: 138 Eagle Street, Albany. The current 39-room mansion was built around a privately owned 10-room house that was constructed in 1856. Sam Tilden was the first of New York's governors to live in the mansion, beginning in 1875. The mansion has undergone some "greening up" with the use of solar panels and other measures to curb energy consumption. To schedule tours by appointment, call 473-7521.

Historic Cherry Hill: 523½ S. Pearl Street, Albany, 434-4791. Cherry Hill houses more than 20,000 objects from the Van Rensselaer–Rankin families. This adorable yellow home also comes complete with the story of lust, betrayal, and murder. Who needs more? (The book *Murder at Cherry Hill* is available at Cherry Hill and the Albany Visitors Center.)

The Home Savings Bank Building: 11 N. Pearl Street, Albany. At the time of its construction in 1927, the Home Savings Bank was, at 19 stories high, the tallest building in Albany. Within one year, the Alfred E. Smith building surpassed it. The Home Savings Bank remains one of the most interesting old banks in Albany because of the terra cotta and gold-colored art deco designs on its top. We always wondered what Spanish conquistadors and Sioux Indians had to do with Albany history, which is nothing by the way, but the sculptor who designed the frieze, Rene Paul Chambellan, one of the most popular art deco designers of the time, didn't care in the least whether the artwork was truly symbolic to this area as long as it looked really cool. Which it does. It has not been a bank for a long time and is currently just office space—really nice office space.

The Hudson River/Hudson River Way: The Hudson River begins at Lake Tear of the Clouds on the southwest slope of Mount Marcy in the Adirondacks, and flows for 315 miles. The 160 miles of navigable water north of Manhattan brought Henry Hudson to what became Albany. Although the river was named for Hudson, no one called it that until late in the 1800s; prior to that, it was known as the North River. (The Delaware was the South River). Recorded history of the area begins here in about 1300 AD and is based on legends of the Lenni Lenape Indians, who were searching for a river that flowed both ways, which the Hudson does because it is an estuary, a tidal river that has both fresh and salt water. Steamboats once traveled up and down the river to bring people back and forth from New York City as well as to get them to Troy. From the Albany waterfront, you could look up the hill to the capitol. That is, until Interstate 787 and the Empire State Plaza came to town with their massive highway maze blotting out the entire view. Thankfully, the Hudson River Way was built in 2002, and now you can actually get to the riverfront to enjoy its beauty. The River Way brings you over the highway to miles of hiking and bicycling trails, an amphitheater for warm-weather music, and a breathtaking view of one of the most beautiful rivers in the world.

New York State Capitol: Capitol Hill, Albany, 474-2418 (tour info). If you live here and haven't taken the tour then do it. It's free and happens Monday through Saturday, unless one of those is a major holiday. This building cost $25 million and took more than 30 years (1867–1899) to build. It is very impressive and has its share of cool stories, with ghosts galore. The detail is amazing, right down to the 17 steps in the back and 77 in the front making the year 1777, which is New York's year of statehood. The Million Dollar Staircase was designed by Henry Hobson

Richardson, one of the four architects who worked on the building. The statue in front is of Civil War General Philip Sheridan and his horse, Rienzi. The city historian says Sheridan was born in Albany, but some suggest his mother was in Ohio at the time, which would make his birth somewhat extraordinary.

Nipper: 991 Broadway, Albany. The 28-foot-high Nipper is the last remaining large statue of the RCA/Victor dog. It has been sitting since 1954 in its current location, where it marked the top of the RTA Company, which distributed RCA products. The Arnoff Moving and Storage Company has taken loving care of this famous landmark for years, but decided to sell the building, pooch and all, in 2014. Hopefully his next owner will be as kind. The real Nipper, so named for his penchant for biting the ankles of passersby, died in 1895. Our Nipper looks down on the site where the last patroon of Albany lived: the Van Rensselaer estate and manor were there until 1893.

The Palace Theatre: 19 Clinton Avenue (at North Pearl Street), Albany, 465-3334. This theater opened in October 1931 and was considered one of the jewels in the RKO (Radio Keith Orpheum, in case you were wondering) chain. It had a successful run as a movie/vaudeville theater through the 1940s, but as was common in much of the area, business declined and the theater failed. It closed by 1969, when it was sold to the city of Albany to be used as a civic auditorium. The murals, plasterwork, chandelier, and the overall historic significance of the Palace put it on the National Register of Historic Places in 1979. The 2,800-seat auditorium became known as a concert venue, and also is home to the Albany Symphony Orchestra. Recent renovations have really made the theater shine again, and movies are once again being shown here. Check the website, www.palacealbany.com, for the theater's excellent upcoming season.

Quackenbush House: 25 Quackenbush Square, Albany. Wouter Quackenbush was a brick maker who, in 1736, built a very nice house *out of bricks!* It used to be known as the oldest Dutch house in Albany, but a few years ago another house dating back to 1732 was uncovered near the Greyhound station on Broadway. Quackenbush House is still the nicest, almost-oldest Dutch house in the city. It is coincidentally located in Quackenbush Square. The original foundation is believed to date back to the 1600s. Across the exit ramp behind it was where Mr. Quackenbush's son distilled rum; his vats were dug up when they started to excavate for the new DEC building. His son changed his name to Quackenboss. The original house was home not only to generations of Quackenbushes, but to bars, a hardware store, French restaurants, and now The Olde English Pub and Pantry, a nice pub with a small menu of very good English pub food. Quackenbush Square is located at the corner of Clinton and Broadway, and may not appear on your GPS.

St. Joseph's Church: Ten Broeck Street, Albany. Patrick Keely (famous for his designs of Catholic churches) designed the gothic St. Joseph's, which was completed in 1860. St. Joseph's was built to serve the growing Irish population. When the Irish neighborhood was demolished for the Empire State Plaza and the residents headed for the suburbs, St. Joseph's no longer had the congregation to sustain it. It was sold and leased back to the church, which had its last service in 1993. The church was then sold to a private family who had plans to turn the building into a club or disco. The building was rapidly deteriorating when the city of Albany took it over. In 2003, the city transferred the property to the Historic Albany Foundation, which then worked tirelessly to stabilize the building. In 2013, Historic Albany turned the church back over to the city after they were unable to agree on a proper tenant. Here's hoping the city can keep on top of this one before we lose it for good.

St. Mary's Roman Catholic Church: 10 Lodge Street, Albany, 462-4254. Incorporated on October 6, 1789, St. Mary's is Albany's oldest Catholic church, and the second oldest in New York state. This is its third edifice, designed by Albany architect Charles Nichols and built in 1867 (the second was designed by Hooker). In 1895, under the eye of Father Clarence Walworth, St. Mary's became the first church to have electricity. He also was responsible for the installation of the 18-foot Archangel Gabriel that sits on top of the church. With each 100 years, major renovations and additions have been made. In 1896, in addition to electricity, the ceiling and upper wall murals were painted. In 1997–98, the interior walls were restored and the gilding redone.

St. Peter's Episcopal Church: 107 State Street, Albany, 434-3502. When the English took over from the Dutch in the 1600s, they built their own church at the top and in the middle of State Street. Eventually, things had to get out of the road, and St. Peter's was built in its present location. This is the third edifice, of which the foundation was laid on St. Peter's Day in 1859. There are beautiful memorial windows throughout the church, and the first window to use flesh tone for human beings is in here, too. L. C. Tiffany spent years during the 1880s developing the chemistry to give glass a more painterly palette, and it is one of his windows, first on the right, that shows off this new technology. The mosaic floor is beautiful, and the gargoyles outside are great. Underneath the entryway is the body of Gen. Lord Howe, an English officer killed in the French and Indian War. He was killed in early July but couldn't be shipped back to England for burial. He was a great friend of Philip Schuyler's, and it was Schuyler who brought his body back from Ticonderoga and arranged to have it buried under the church, which makes Howe the only British lord to be buried in America.

Schuyler Mansion: 32 Catherine Street (Catharine Van Rensselaer was the first Mrs. Philip Schuyler), Albany, 434-0834. The mansion was built between 1761 and 1765 and is home to many family artifacts. If you're not from the area and/or didn't make the obligatory first-grade trip to this site, then be sure to visit it now. There have been some interesting tours of late, which offer a glimpse of the not-so-boring lives of Albany's founding fathers.

Spectrum 8 Theatre: 290 Delaware Avenue, Albany, 449-8995. This is the best movie theater around. The original owners took over its present location, the former Delaware Theater, in 1983. It now houses eight small theaters of assorted sizes that show an assortment of independent and foreign films, semi-blockbusters, and the occasional real blockbuster if it's good enough. The snack bar sells popcorn with *real* butter, and great brownies and cookies, with some of their delicious specialties supplied by the local bakery Crisan. The staff is friendly and very cinema savvy. The art displayed is from local artists and/or galleries. And if this isn't enough, there are two parking lots for off-street parking. After 35 years of independent ownership, the Spectrum was sold to Landmark Theatres in the fall of 2015, with the promise they would continue its legacy in stewardship, and also to keep their hands off the popcorn. Check their website for ticket prices.

The State Bank of Albany: 69 State Street, Albany. Currently the Bank of America, this bank is the oldest in the city and the oldest banking building to be continuously run as a bank in the United States. Originally the N.Y. State National Bank, it was founded in 1803, and designed by up-and-coming architect Philip Hooker. The building has been greatly modified over the past 200 years, but the entrance and the brass railing are from the original design. Inside, there are 10 wall murals measuring 12 feet wide by more than 6 feet high, depicting scenes from Albany's past. These include glimpses of the original Mohicans, Henry Hudson's arrival, the building of Fort Orange, and even a painting of Hooker presenting his plans for the design of the bank. The paintings were done by David Lithgow, the same artist who did the ceiling in the Alfred E. Smith building, the 14 murals in the Milne Building of the University of Albany downtown campus, and tons of smaller paintings, some of which are at the Albany Institute of History and Art. You can actually go inside this building and see the murals because it is open to the public during banking hours.

The New York State Education Building: 89 Washington Avenue, Albany, across from the capitol. The building was the vision of Dr. Andrew Draper, New York's first commissioner of education. He wanted to build a temple to education, and after a design competition, the Palmer and Hornbostle architectural firm was hired to do just that. Construction began in 1908 and was completed in 1911, although the building was not dedicated until the following year. The 36-column colonnade across the front is the longest in the United States and one of the longest in the world. Originally, the State Museum and State Library both were housed upstairs. You could have come to visit the Cohoes mastodon with his furry friend until 1976, when it was dismantled and put into storage at the new State Museum at Empire State Plaza. (He's up again in the South Hall lobby at the museum.) The State Education building has an amazing rotunda with a 70-foot chandelier hanging in it. There are murals, vaulted ceilings, readings rooms—all pretty outstanding. But unless you work in the building you won't get past the lobby; there is a brochure with pictures available at the information desk downstairs. Charles Keck designed the electroliers (lamp fixtures) that are outside the building. He used his nieces and nephews as the models for the studious kids sitting around them. For its centennial in 2012, there were some tours available, but not since. You can stop by and admire the grandeur of it all, at least from the outside.

SUNY Plaza: State and Broadway, Albany (originally the headquarters of the Delaware and Hudson [D&H] Railroad). In 1912, Arnold William Brunner was asked by the Mayor of Albany to draw up a series of plans to improve and beautify the city. One of the first was to design a plaza with a suitable building for the railroad company that would block out the unpleasant view of tracks and trains without hindering the workings of the railroad. Marcus T. Reynolds, one of Albany's notable architects, designed the beautiful D&H Railroad building, which was to surround a plaza made up of patched-together plots off State Street. Brunner tentatively called this "The Plaza" and hoped "that a name will be officially adopted that will be distinctly Albanian and intimately related to the city's history." Nope. It stayed The Plaza and now is known as SUNY Plaza. A book called *Studies for Albany*, published in 1914, outlines all of Brunner's plans for the city: sunken gardens! A grand city gate! Parks! Monuments! Beauty everywhere! We got the building and the plaza. We really like it though. This building is cited as one of the most popular downtown buildings; what's not to like about a gigantic fairy castle along the river? Reynolds also designed the nine-foot weathervane of the *Half Moon* (Henry Hudson's ship in 1609) that sits on top of the building, which weighs around 400 pounds and is the largest working weathervane in the United States (and one of the largest weathervanes in the world). It has carvings of things relating to almost everyone who played a part in Albany's history, including beavers. D&H Railroad sold the building to the State University of New York in the 1960s, and it is now the university's central administration building.

Ten Broeck Mansion: 9 Ten Broeck Place, Albany, 436-9826. Built to replace the original Ten Broeck home, which burned down in the fire of 1793, the Ten Broeck Mansion is a lovely Federal-style house with beautiful gardens. It hosts haunted Halloween tours and a great Christmas holiday house. In the summer, kids can dig up the backyard in archaeology camp.

Union Station: Broadway between Steuben and Columbia Streets, Albany. Now the Peter D. Kiernan Plaza, Union Station opened on

December 17, 1900. It was designed by the Shepley, Rutan, and Coolidge firm (successors to H. H. Richardson) and built by the Norcross Brothers. It took about two years to complete. The carved eagle and figures surrounding the clock took three months alone. Hundreds of trains passed through Albany each week. New York Central Railroad had plans to abandon it when parts of its rail yards were needed for the construction of the I-787 highway. The last train left the station on December 29, 1968, almost exactly 68 years after its opening. Governor Nelson Rockefeller bought the building with state funds in 1966; however, from 1968 to 1984 it was left to rot on the city's landscape, in part because there were no funds to do anything with it. Mayor Erastus Corning wanted the building preserved for sentimental reasons as well as historic ones (his great-grandfather had founded the New York Central Railroad). Finally, Norstar Bancorp chairman Peter D. Kiernan brought the city an acceptable plan. The bank would buy and completely renovate the old Union Station, and make it its headquarters; it was then renamed the Peter D. Kiernan Plaza. Renovations began in 1984, the building reopened in 1986, and then Bank of America (formerly Norstar) abandoned it once again. Most recently, it has been swallowed up by the SUNY College of Nanoscale Science and Engineering for its Smart Cities Technology Innovation Center, or SCiTI.

United Traction Building: 600 Broadway, Albany. This is another one of those beautiful buildings designed by Marcus T. Reynolds (SUNY Plaza). The United Traction Company was a consolidation of the Albany Railway, the Troy City Railway, and the Watervliet Turnpike and Railroad Company. The companies signed the merger on December 30, 1899, the same year the new headquarters was built. United Traction was plagued by strikes, most notably the strike of May 1901, in which 3,000 militiamen were called in to subdue the strikers. This was followed by strikes in 1918 and 1921—the last one lasting a year and immortalized in the movie *Ironweed*. The last trolley run in Troy was in 1933, and in Albany it was in 1946. The bus system eventually became the Capital District Transportation Authority (CDTA). The United Traction Building became the Pieter Schuyler Building (named after Albany's first mayor) and now mostly houses law offices.

Washington Park: Between Madison Avenue, Willett, State, and South Lake streets, Albany. This is a really beautiful city park that hosts a number of events throughout the year, including Tulipfest in May. It is an 81-acre park designed by John Bogart and John Cuyler based on plans by Frederick Law Olmsted, who designed New York's Central Park. (Bogart had worked for Olmsted.) There are walking paths throughout; tennis courts; some really great sculptures, including the one of Moses (by J. Massey Rhind, the same artist who did the Philip Schuyler in front of City Hall); the Henry Johnson memorial at the southeastern corner on Henry Johnson Boulevard; the Robert Burns statue; and the Lakehouse, which is where you will find free musical theater in the summer.

Troy—On the Edge of Greatness

We love Troy. Maybe it's not that close to greatness, but it's almost been there. It has stupendous architecture, Tiffany windows, a clear view of the Hudson, an outstanding year-round farmer's market, coffee shops on every corner, and a Dinosaur Bar-B-Que. It also has a population that loves it. It's been working soooo hard on a comeback; maybe its time has come. Troy is lovingly known as the place where Henry Hudson turned around, but it proved itself to be a place of invention and industry.

Before it was Troy, it was just a farming community included in the massive 800,000-acre Van Rensselaer patroonship. In 1791, the "Town of Troy" was laid out, and by 1816 it was chartered as the city of Troy. Early on, it was mainly just a way station for the produce and meats from Vermont to be shipped down the Hudson, but during the War of 1812 it was also made famous by "Uncle Sam" Wilson, who was a meat-packer for the US troops. In 1823, with the opening of the Erie Canal, Troy now had access to two canal systems and the Hudson River for shipping goods.

The invention of the detachable collar in 1825 and its production in Troy made Troy one of the fastest growing and richest cities in the country. The collar industry also saw the rise of the first female labor union, founded by Kate Mullany. Henry Burden's iron and nail factory rivaled the factories in Pennsylvania. During the Civil War, the H. Burden and Sons factory produced close to one million horseshoes a week to keep up with demand. In 1821, the Troy Female Seminary opened (in 1895, it was renamed the Emma Willard School for Girls, after its founder). The Rensselaer School (later Rensselaer Polytechnic Institute) was established in 1824.

Troy was plagued with fires throughout its early history—1820, 1852, 1854—but the really big one came in 1862, and wiped out a good chunk of downtown. It was completely rebuilt in six months, but this time in the grand Victorian style.

Troy's geography made it a bootlegger's dream during Prohibition. Alcohol was shipped down from Canada and off-loaded to one of Troy's many red-light establishments. Troy became known worldwide for its red-light district, which was frequented by businessmen, students, and soldiers passing through on their way to war. After World War II, the city's fortunes changed as the shirt business that grew out of the collar business moved south, the steel industries moved to Pennsylvania, and the city seemed to fall asleep. Nothing changed; no urban renewal, no renovations. Everything from the golden age was left untouched. This was a good thing. The movies *Ironweed*, *Age of Innocence*, *The Bostonians*, *Scent of a Woman*, and *The Time Machine* all used Troy's past as a backdrop. It is also what is attracting a new generation of Trojans. Troy's motto is "Ilium fuit, Troja est": Ilium was, Troy is. Well, it will be.

Paper Canoes Were Made Here, Too!

Everyone knows Troy was famous for its detachable-collar, steel, and iron industries, and even as the birthplace of "Uncle Sam." But most people have forgotten or have never heard of Elisha Waters' world-renowned paper-boat company, which was right in Troy.

Elisha Waters was an interesting man. He was born in Vermont in 1815, and his family moved to Troy in 1831. His first jobs were with druggists, where he did very well. He opened his own drugstore in 1838, concocting all kinds of medicines, as well as inks and dyes. If you're a bottle collector, you might have an E. Waters ink jar in your collection. By 1852, business was booming and he needed more and better packing materials to move his goods. This inspired his paper-box business. His boxes were so good other businesses requested them, and he slowly got out of the drugstore business, going fully into box making by 1858. Ammunition for the Union troops was shipped in his boxes during the Civil War. He obtained a number of patents for paper products during what was called "the age of paper."

The paper-boat business started by happenstance. Elisha's teenage son George had been invited to a costume ball, and not having the money to buy the elaborate mask he wanted, he borrowed it, and basically made a lightweight cast of it with paper and glue in the family factory. The idea for a paper boat followed almost immediately. Those were the days of regattas and intercollegiate boat racing, and everyone wanted faster, lighter racing shells. The Waters took an old cedar shell and started layering Manila paper and shellac to form their boat. When dry, they could lift it off the form and strengthen it with wood bulkheads and inwales. The boat was 20 percent lighter than its wooden counterpart and almost seamless, letting it glide across the river. In 1868, Waters received his first patents for paper boats for both the United States and Canada. Their first boat was christened *The Experiment*. With the invention of the Fourdrinier Machine, which could produce continuous rolls of paper, boats were easier to build with an even thinner shell. When Cornell beat out 12 other colleges racing a paper boat on Saratoga Lake in 1875, followed by a clean sweep of the Centennial Regatta in 1876 by paper boats, it became clear that paper boats were here to stay. Well, at least for 30 years or so.

Waters, always inventive, followed up paper canoes with paper observatories, one of which was installed in the Proudfit building at Rensselaer Polytechnic Institute, with others at West Point, Columbia, and the old Brooklyn Poly. The RPI dome lasted 20 years; the West Point dome was dismantled in 1958. The Waters' paper-boat business came to an abrupt end in 1901 when George accidentally set the factory on fire while applying the finishing touches on a shell bound for Syracuse. Nothing could be saved, and the insurance was not nearly enough to rebuild. George died within a year of the fire, and his father soon after in 1904. The patents for all of their boats (including a whaling boat!) and domes were kept by George's brother Clarence, which prevented others from building the paper boats, so the process became forgotten. In more recent years, amateur boat builders have begun experimenting with the Waters' methods using updated adhesives and papers. Check out duckworksmagazine.com to bring out the boat builder in you.

A wonderful book published in 1878, called *The Voyage of the Paper Canoe* by Nathaniel Bishop, chronicles his 2,500-mile trip from Quebec to Cedar Keys, Florida, in 1874. He started his voyage in a traditional wooden boat, but in transit, heard about Waters' canoes and decided to complete his voyage in one of them. The first 400 miles, he had an assistant to help him, but with his new 58-pound canoe, he could continue along solo. He traveled from Troy to Florida, describing everything in colorful detail. He had only one mishap, in the Delaware Bay, but his paper canoe received only a few scratches where a wooden boat would have been destroyed. Apart from the details of the navigation, his descriptions of American life and the people he met shortly after the

Civil War are an interesting glance into our past. You can read it online or look for a hard copy on eBay.

Did You Know?

Right in the middle of Troy, at 300 Broadway, is the **Tech Valley Center of Gravity.** This is a membership organization where you can get access to all of the tools you need to build your dreams. It is fabulous! The THINQubator is where kids can find out just how much fun science is.

Places to Visit in Troy

Burden Iron Works Museum: 1 East Industrial Parkway, Troy, 274-5267. Housed in the old brick offices of the Burden Iron Works, the museum is open 10 a.m. to 6 p.m. weekdays, usually by appointment. You should call ahead so they can turn the heat on before you get there. The building itself is a really nice Romanesque-style structure (see H. H. Richardson under the Famous Who), and was built between 1881 and 1882. It houses artifacts and information from Troy's industrial past. Burden was known for its massive horseshoe production during the Civil War, but earlier, it was the invention of his Burden Spike Machine (patented in 1839), which could make a complete spike with head and point, that helped build the railroads of America. The museum not only celebrates the Burden Factory contributions, but all the other local factories that produced stoves, bells, collars, and even parts for the USS *Monitor*. For more information, visit www.hudsonmohawkgateway.org.

Charles Nalle Plaque: On the building on the north corner of State Street between 1st and 2nd Streets, Troy. On April 27, 1860, citizens of Troy fought to keep Charles Nalle a free man. After escaping slavery in Virginia, and settling in Troy, he was turned in to authorities (by Horatio Averill of Averill Park fame) in compliance with the odious Fugitive Slave Act. While Nalle was being handed over to federal marshals, a visiting Harriet Tubman and the local vigilance committee went into action and managed to get him away from the marshals and across the river to West Troy (Watervliet). He was recaptured there, held, bloodied from his shackles, but again freed as the door was broken down and he was dragged to freedom through a hail of gunfire. He was then taken to and hidden in Niskayuna until his freedom could be purchased for $650. He returned to Troy, and eventually reunited with his wife and children, never telling any of them the tale of his rescue. There are many books about his story; *Freeing Charles* by Scott Christianson is a good one. The plaque marks the spot of the first part of his escape.

Frear's Troy Cash Bazaar: Corner of Fulton and 3rd streets, Troy. William Henry Frear began his career as a salesman and businessman extraordinaire in 1859 in Troy at the age of 18. In 1865, he opened his first dry-goods store with partner Slyvanus Haverly in Troy. In that year Haverly and Frear made over $100,000. Soon, Frear's former employer, John Flagg, joined the growing operation which then became Flagg, Haverly & Frear. By 1874, he had bought out both partners (Frear at last) and renamed the store Frear's Troy Cash Bazaar, which became world famous and eventually housed more than 53 different departments under one roof. In 1897 he moved the still-expanding store into a structure he had built on the corner of Fulton and 3rd. Frear coined the phrase "Satisfaction guaranteed or your money cheerfully refunded." He died in 1911, and the store closed by the beginning of the 1960s, but it has been carefully restored for commercial and office use. The original wrought-iron-and-marble staircase and glass dome are absolutely gorgeous! You can access the bazaar during the week by going up to the second floor of the Troy Atrium and going through the doorway over the CVS. You can also go in through the door to the Frear Building on 3rd Street, take the elevator up to the second floor, and get to the staircase that way. Go see it.

Frear Park: 217 Lavin Court, or Frear Park Road, right off Oakwood Avenue, Troy, 274-7275. This beautiful, now-247-acre park was donated to the city by the Frear Family in 1917 on the condition they call it Frear Park, name a street across from the park Frear Avenue, let the family build a gateway entrance off Oakwood, and maintain the fountain at that entrance. Done, done, done, and done. The fountain that graces the entrance was completed in 1924 and is still a wonderful sight to see on your way into the park. The Frear family ran Frear's Troy Cash Bazaar, the building still a landmark in downtown Troy. There is an 18-hole golf course and a clubhouse restaurant to go with it, tennis courts, softball fields, ice skating rink, and some really nice nature trails that take you by the park's two lakes, named for Frear family members Wright and Bradley. Our family has always loved sledding here in the winter. Open year round. Enjoy.

The Gasholder House: 5th Avenue at Jefferson Street in Troy's Little Italy. Next time you're down picking up your pizza at DeFazio's, take a couple of blocks' detour to Jefferson Street. At the corner of 5th, look past the trees and behold one of the coolest buildings in Troy. Built in

1873 by the Troy Gas Light Company and designed by Frederick A. Sabbaton, the Gasholder House was one example of a common sight in the Northeast, where manufactured coal gas was stored and then used to light the city streets. This one was in service until the 1920s and is one of only a handful still around. It is really odd to see a huge round building with a cupola on top just sitting at the end of a residential street. The iron holding tanks were sold for scrap in the 1930s, and the building has been used mostly for storage since then. Marquise Productions, a Troy based "contemporary circus productions company," has used it for a series of performances in the last couple of years. Check them out at www.marquiseproductions.com.

Ilium Building: 400 Fulton Street, Troy. Situated next to the Fulton Street Gallery is one of Troy's first skyscrapers, a whole five stories high. The Cummings architectural firm designed the Ilium Building. It has detailed stonework all the way around, and a very nice entryway. We were told that its elevator is the oldest in the city. It certainly feels like it when it tries to climb to the upper floors. The Ilium is home to a number of artists who rent studio space upstairs. Check to see if they're open during a Troy Night Out (last Friday of every month), and be amazed.

Oakwood Cemetery: 186 Oakwood Avenue (Route 40) off Hoosick Street, 272-7520, Troy. The cemetery was incorporated in 1848, and approximately 60,000 people are buried here. It is one of the most beautiful cemeteries in the country, with more than 400 wooded acres with five lakes, waterfalls, and an unbelievable 100-mile panoramic view of the Hudson River. You can see from the Catskills to the Adirondacks from the bluffs in this cemetery. The Gardner Earl Memorial Chapel and Crematorium alone is worth the visit here. This chapel was built in 1888–89 by the Earls, who made their fortune in Troy's detachable collar business, as a memorial to their only son Gardner. During a trip to Europe a few years before his death, Gardner became very interested in cremation, which was virtually unheard of in this country. When he died, as per his request, he was cremated in Buffalo, the location of the closest crematory. In his honor, the Earls built the Earl Chapel with the first crematory in eastern New York. The first cremation took place in 1890. Inside there are eight Tiffany windows, marble mosaics, Maitland Armstrong stained glass windows, hand-carved oak, and custom bronze work. You can take a virtual tour of this chapel on the Oakwood Cemetery web page. Many famous people are buried here, including "Uncle Sam" Wilson, Emma Willard, and Russell Sage. There is a nice memorial monument for Robert Ross, who believed in voting rights for all, and was murdered while poll watching on Election Day, March 6, 1894, by a gang of repeat voters (part of Troy's then-Democratic machine).

Prospect Park: 65 Prospect Park Road, off Congress Street, Troy, 235-7761. At the turn of the 20th century, Troy felt it was time for a really good city park. Brooklyn had just about completed its fabulous Prospect Park, and Troy city fathers thought it was a good model for them. They purchased land from the Warren family (part of this land once was owned by "Uncle Sam" Wilson and his brother Eb), and hired Garnet

D. Baltimore, who had recently become the first African American to graduate from R.P.I., to design the park. Troy's "Warren Park" opened in 1902, well before it was actually finished. The name didn't quite fit, so they held a contest to rename it. Prospect Park was the winner. An epic history of the park was written by local historian Don Rittner, which you can read on his blog at the *Times Union*. Currently, the park is 80 acres, and includes 14 well-maintained tennis courts, handball courts, basketball courts, and a playground. There still is the original swimming pool, closed a long time now, and a little spooky looking with weeds growing inside it. There is an overlook where you can see the name "TROY" in gigantic stone letters and a view of the city. There are also some history markers at the overlook where you can catch up on Troy's past. Open mid-April to mid-November.

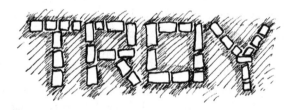

Rensselaer County Historical Society and Museum: 57 2nd Street, Troy, 272-7232. The Hart-Cluett House and the Carr Building in Troy's historic district house the collections of the Historical Society. The Hart-Cluett House is a house museum and is open for tours the second Saturday of the month, March through November, or by appointment. The Carr Building houses the society's art, costume, and militaria collections, as well as its library. Have a question about Troy's past? They just might have the answer here. The collections are always changing, so stop by Thursday through Saturday, noon to 5 p.m. Good to call first. Check the society's website, http://www.rchsonline.org/about/, for more information.

Rensselaer Polytechnic Institute (RPI): In his later years, Stephen Van Rensselaer, the last patroon of Albany, established the Rensselaer School in 1824 "for the purpose of instructing persons, who may choose to apply themselves, in the application of science to the common purposes of life." He co-founded the school with Amos Eaton, who became its first senior professor. (Eaton had an unbelievably tragic life up to this point, including being sent to prison for life after he was framed for forgery during the very hectic and shady land-dealing time of the Erie Canal construction. Governor DeWitt Clinton pardoned him unconditionally when the evidence against him was found to be false.) At Rensselaer, women were also admitted in courses of study that prepared them for a teaching career. Eight actually graduated in 1835. If you wanted to learn science, Emma Willard's Troy Female Seminary was just down the hill, and there Eaton taught science to the women (Emma Willard had previously attended a number of Eaton's lectures, which he invited both men and women to attend).

The Rensselaer School began in a building called the Old Bank Place, which was built in 1801 and also housed Troy's first bank, the Farmer's Bank. The building, later bought by Amos Eaton, had classrooms, laboratories, a library, living space for students, and even an observatory. From 1834 through 1841, the school (now the Rensselaer Institute) leased the mansion built by Troy founder Jacob Van der Heyden, then returned to Old Bank Place. Eaton died in 1842; the Rensselaer Institute stayed in the bank building until 1844. After the school was bumped from the bank, the city of Troy turned over property known as the Infant School at State and 6th to Rensselaer, which stayed there until it was destroyed during the great fire of 1862. At this point, Rensselaer Polytechnic Institute, as it was now known, started to get serious and built its own building, called the Main Building, in 1864. Alas, fire took this one as well in 1904, and the property was turned over to Troy. In 1906, after Russell Sage's death (see below), his wife, Margaret Olivia Slocum Sage, donated $1 million for the construction of the Russell Sage Laboratory. In 1907, RPI completed the Approach, that massive granite staircase you can see looking up to the campus from downtown. The campus has continually grown, building new buildings and absorbing old ones, including the purportedly haunted West Hall, built in 1868, which was the Troy Hospital built to aid Irish cholera victims. The new EMPAC (Experimental Media and Performing Arts Center) opened October 3, 2008.

The Hirsch Observatory on campus opens its view to the universe free to the public on Saturdays from 8 to 10 p.m., February to mid-November. RPI is one of the oldest engineering schools in North America. George W. G. Ferris (of the Ferris wheel) graduated from RPI in 1881.

Russell Sage College and the Magnificent Margaret Olivia Slocum Sage: Russell Sage College was founded in 1916 using the buildings formerly of the Emma Willard School, which had moved to its new campus up on Pawling Avenue in 1910. The original Emma Willard School was called the Troy Female Seminary and was founded by Emma Willard, who was certain that women were smart enough to learn geography and math just like the boys. One of her students was Margaret Slocum, a suffragist.

Margaret married the wealthy financier Russell Sage when she was in her early 40s; this was his second marriage. He was mean and miserly, but very rich, and when he died in 1906, Margaret Olivia Slocum Sage inherited upwards of $70 million and started giving it away almost immediately. She put her husband's name on everything from the Russell Sage Foundation, the Russell Sage Laboratory at Rensselaer Polytechnic Institute, to Russell Sage College itself. No one is really sure whether she did this as some inside joke that only she knew, or whether it was just another aspect of her generosity. The original college operated under Emma Willard's charter, but eventually got its own. It was strictly a women's college, offering a liberal arts education. Men were admitted to the Troy campus during World War II only as an emergency measure. In 1949, the Albany campus opened, offering men and women two- and four-year degrees. This became the Sage Junior College of Albany and now Sage College of Albany. The Troy campus houses the amazing New York State Theater Institute (NYSTI), which is located in the Schacht Fine Arts Center.

As well as building the new Emma Willard School and renovating the old one and turning it into the Russell Sage College, Mrs. Sage donated money to many colleges including Yale, Princeton, and Cornell universities, and piles of it to Rensselaer Polytechnic Institute. The Russell Sage Foundation continues to fund projects that impact social and living conditions throughout the United States. She even bought an island in the Gulf of Mexico as a home for wild birds. WOW!!

Troy Savings Bank Music Hall: 30 2nd Street, Troy, 273-0038. In a structure built in 1875 as the headquarters for the now-absorbed Troy Savings Bank, the top floor houses an acoustic marvel of a music hall. The seats have been as uncomfortable as the sound is good; even with the padding added in recent years, they are still hard to sit still in. Luckily, most of the concerts will make you forget all about that. Beside the original frescoes, the Odell Opus 190 organ installed in the music hall in 1890 is up and playing again. The organ was built in 1882 for William Belden, a rich man from Manhattan, who sold it to the music hall in 1889. When Troy slid into its decline of the 1960s, no one had the money or inclination to support the arts and the music hall, and its organ fell into disrepair. The Troy Savings Bank Revitalization Committee, founded by a group of private citizens in 1979, took the steps that led to the formation of the not-for-profit Troy Savings Bank Music Hall Corporation, which saved the venue. By 2006, the organ was back in playable condition. In 1989, the Troy Savings Bank Music Hall was named a national historic landmark. Check for upcoming concerts at www.troymusichall.org/.

Troy Public Library (aka William Howard Hart Memorial Library): 100 2nd Street, Troy, 274-7071. Mary E. Hart built the library as a memorial to her husband, William Howard Hart, in 1897. Designed by architects J. Stewart Barney and Henry Otis Chapman in the American Renaissance style, this is one spiffy building. However, for all of its grandeur, there was never enough money for the library to fully operate. It changed its name to the Troy Public Library in 1903 in hopes of attracting some municipal funding. That never really worked either. Even so, it has managed to stay open as a free public library for more than 100 years. This is the only library in which you will find a Tiffany window over the circulation desk. Frederick Wilson designed the window, which portrays Venetian scholar Aldus Manutius (1450–1515). On the upper right corner of the window is this quote from Isidore of Saville: "Study as if you were to live forever and live as if you were to die tomorrow." Sounds like a good idea.

The Troy Waterfront Farmer's Market: Saturdays, year round, 312-5749. From November to April it is located at the Uncle Sam Atrium from 9 a.m. to 2 p.m. From May to October it is in the middle of Troy on River Street, also from 9 a.m. to 2 p.m. As of this writing, they are looking to build permanent digs on the riverfront within the next few years. What can we say? This is the best farmer's market around. You can find fresh produce year round from local farmers, as well as fresh cheeses, baked goods, and nonhomogenized farm-fresh milk in glass bottles from Battenkill Valley Creamery. There is always music, hot food, and hot fair-trade coffee. You can find local wines, honey, art, and fresh pesto. Make this part of your Saturday routine. It will make your life better.

Van Schaick Mansion: 1 Van Schaick Avenue, Cohoes, 235-2699. Built in 1735 by the Van Schaick family, the mansion has many connections to the Revolutionary War. In gearing up for the war, the family was asked to lend General Horatio Gates $10,000 in gold for war supplies. Congress never repaid this debt, saying Gates was not authorized to borrow it, so the government had no need to repay it! Tours are monthly or by appointment.

Watervliet Arsenal: 1 Buffington Street, Watervliet, 266-5111. The Watervliet Arsenal is the oldest continually running arsenal in the United States and is still producing much of the artillery for the United States Army. It was built in 1813 to support the War of 1812 on a 12-acre site along the Hudson River. It now covers 142 acres and includes the Benet Laboratories. In 1887, it became known as America's cannon factory, and cannons remain its principal product. In 1988, it opened up the grounds for its 175th anniversary, and you could see the old living quarters and the beautiful greenhouse built in 1903. It had a wonderful museum housed in the "Iron Building," a prefabricated cast-iron building erected in 1859 to store equipment. The museum had been open for more than 35 years, but due to security concerns it closed in the fall of 2013, and most of its collection was given to other museums.

Did You Know?

Between 1867 and 1917 there was a 42-acre park in Lansingburg between 108th and 110th Streets that housed a 1.5-mile track for harness bicycle and harness chariot racing, as well as pedestrian matches. It was called Rensselaer Park. The famous pedestrian Edward Weston "raced" five others there, but the match was won by an English pedestrian who walked 100 miles in 23 hours and 37 seconds, winning him $300 and an additional $100 for doing it in under 24 hours. The amusement park boasted a 10-seat Ferris wheel, a roller coaster, pony rides, music, sideshows, and fireworks every Thursday night. Tragically, the aviator George L. Newberry crashed during a barnstorming exhibition in front of 20,000 spectators in 1915, and died at a nearby hospital. The park closed in 1917, and the new owner promised to reopen it, but turned it into building lots instead.

Schenectady—The Lights Are Still On

It's no longer a five-hour ride on horseback to Schenectady from Albany, but the King's Highway (Albany calls it Central Avenue, Schenectady calls it State Street) still connects the two formerly stockaded cities. The name is taken from the Mohawk Indian word meaning "land near the pine barrens." Actually, Albany was Schenectady first. Schau-naugh-ta-da was the land "beyond the pines" when you looked over from the Mohawk River, but Fort Orange already had a name it liked, so its residents began using the same name to refer to the land "beyond the pines" from them.

A group led by Arendt Van Curler first settled Schenectady in 1661. Tired of living the patroonship lifestyle, Van Curler petitioned Governor Stuyvesant to allow him to purchase land from the Mohawks so that the settlers could actually own the land they worked on. After wrangling with the powers that be for three years (one result being that they were forbidden to benefit from the fur trade), the group got the go-ahead and divided up their Schenectady into nice little farm, pasture, and home lots. Van Curler was a great friend to the Mohawks who, in turn, were very supportive to the fledgling community. The population grew to approximately 400 people before it all ended in 1690.

On February 8, 1690, a group of French and their Indian allies came down from Canada and attacked a sleeping and unguarded stockade. Fire was set to almost all of the homes, and as their inhabitants ran outside, they were slaughtered. Few escaped, and many were taken prisoner. Symon Schermerhorn is remembered for his famous ride, in which, though wounded, he escaped by horseback to warn the citizens of Albany of a possible attack. A small group of militia under the guidance of Captain Bull traveled to Schenectady the following day to help inter the bodies. The village was nothing but burning embers surrounded by the dead bodies of 60 men, women, and children frozen into the snow.

Only two of the attackers were killed in the battle. The few Albany militia, along with local Mohawks (notably Lawrence the Indian) and Mohicans, followed them back north and killed 17 more.

After such a blow, it seemed difficult to imagine that the town could come back. With much encouragement and help from the Mohawks, the settlement made a slow recovery. In 1765, Schenectady became a borough, and in 1798 it was chartered as the city of Schenectady. During the Revolutionary War years, with the glow of new democracy, the idea of common schooling was becoming an ideal to be achieved. In 1779, Senior Elder John Cuyler of the Dutch Reformed Church in Schenectady introduced a petition to the brand-new New York State Senate to help establish this goal. Being busy with the war and all, the lawmakers set it aside, but it was this petition that began the 16-year process of getting a charter for what would become Union College. (The petition was revived momentarily in 1780 by Governor/General Clinton, who thought "Clinton College" had a nice ring to it, and brought the proposal back to the legislature, where again it was ignored).

In 1784, the Reverend Dirck Romeyn arrived from New Jersey and set about to enact his 12 "measures" for setting up some kind of seminary in Schenectady. This would become the Schenectady Academy (1785), chartered in 1793 (as an academy, not a college—it was considered too small, and lacked sufficient financial backing), with the goal to make it a college. Fund-raising went into overdrive, so that the next time, money would not be an issue in denying Schenectady its college. Meanwhile in Albany, the thought of a college being chartered for *common* people was so appalling that, although late to the game, they too started to solicit funds for their own Albany College to benefit the upper class. (Fund-raising for an Albany-based college was begun in 1792, but no clear plans had been made; the threat of a Schenectady college pushed them to define their plans in quick fashion.)

In 1795, two requests for charters were presented to the New York State Board of Regents: one for Albany College and one for Union College. The Union boosters argued that it was much less expensive to live in Schenectady than Albany, and that Schenectady had "comparatively few fashionable vices." (This had little bearing on the outcome. It was the backing of Albany's own Philip Schuyler—a member of the Board of Regents as well as a million other things, who had given his word to support the Schenectady bid if it met the requirements—that clinched the deal.) Union (an outgrowth of the Schenectady Academy) was given the charter, and the college's official founding day was February 25, 1795. Samuel Fortenbaugh's *In Order to Form a More Perfect Union* (1978) is a really interesting read on how politics, money, and religion came together to create Union.

In the early 1800s, the Watervliet Shakers introduced broomcorn to the Schenectady area. It adapted well to the soil and became a major crop, and broom making a major industry. Schenectady became known as the broom capital of the world. And yet, its city seal is a sheaf of *wheat*. There were more than a dozen broom manufacturers in nearby Glenville alone. (Glenville does celebrate this with broomcorn on its seal.) The Schenectady Locomotive Works had its beginnings in the mid-19th century, and by the 1860s was turning out five to six locomotives per month.

Schenectady's growth was helped by the proximity to the Mohawk River and the Erie Canal, but really took off when, in 1887, Thomas Edison moved his Edison Machine Works here. In 1892, the company became General Electric (GE). George Westinghouse, Jr. invented his rotary engine and air brakes in Schenectady. The American Locomotive Works (ALCO), formed in 1901 by merging a number of smaller companies, including the Schenectady Locomotive Works, and made almost every steam and diesel locomotive that crossed America. (GE pretty much put ALCO out of business with its own diesel-electric locomotives in 1969.) GE still builds locomotives among millions of other things, and today is still one of the largest companies in the world. Once, GE was the largest employer in Schenectady. When most of GE's manufacturing jobs went south or overseas in the 1970s and '80s, Schenectady lost one third of its population. GE always kept a presence here, and in 2010 dedicated $45 million to its renewable energy headquarters, which was based in Schenectady. With the acquisition of France's Alstom SA (a major player in the offshore wind business) in 2015, GE moved the Renewable Energy Headquarters to Paris. GE's onshore wind unit is still based in Schenectady, and one of GE's global research centers is based in Niskayuna.

Schenectady is also a place to visit for a great night out. Proctors, on State Street, continues to present affordable Broadway in downtown, as well as smaller plays, performances, films, and other events in the black-box-styled GE Theatre. During the winter months, Proctors also hosts the wonderful Schenectady Greenmarket (which moves outdoors to the area around city hall May through October). Bow Tie Cinemas Movieland 6, a top-notch movie theater, is a few doors down. Schenectady Light Opera Company, Schenectady Civic Players, the Classic Theater Guild, and Mopco all make downtown their home. The new crop of restaurants in and around State Street offer a great selection for anyone's tastes. Enjoy!

What's on the Tee Vee?

They didn't invent TV in Schenectady, but General Electric's radio picture service, W2XB—eventually WRGB—was one of the first to develop the science of broadcast programming.

In 1884, while a student in Germany, Paul Gottlieb Nipkow patented the idea for an electro-mechanical TV system using what would become known as a Nipkow disk. In really basic terms, it involves a lamp shining through a spinning disk with a set number of holes in it (the patent called for 30), casting light on a subject. This light is reflected back to a photo cell, which is read as fluctuating electric current and is then sent as radio waves. It's then received the same way, the electrical signal going through a neon lamp, then the rotating Nipkow disk, which then sends its flickering image onto a tiny screen. Nipkow never made a prototype, and it wasn't until 1926 that a Scottish inventor transmitted a moving image using this electro-mechanical method—Nipkow's.

In 1928, GE stepped up to the plate by establishing W2XB, an experimental electro-mechanical broadcast station from its labs in Schenectady. The same year, its scientists designed a television receiver with a whopping big three-inch screen. They never manufactured these tiny sets, but *Popular Science Monthly*—your go-to, you-can-build-anything magazine—published plans for one in 1931. GE used two radio transmitters for these early images. Visuals were broadcast by W2XB, and sound on radio station WGY. On September 11, 1928, they aired the first television drama in America, called *The Queen's Messenger*, which people watched on their tiny homemade TVs. The screens were so small that they broadcasted only the faces and hands of the actors. Four actors were used, two for their faces, and two for their hands. Although the technology was very limited at this point, WGY started broadcasting television programs three days a week: Tuesday, Thursday, and Friday from 12:30 to 1 p.m.

The year 1928 also saw the start of the New York City station W2XBS, developed by RCA, which would become NBC. RCA's radio tower on the Empire State Building could send programming to GE's tower, which was on a mountaintop in the Helderbergs. This was the start of a very long relationship WRGB had with RCA/NBC. It lasted until 1981, when WRGB became an affiliate of CBS. With the development of all-electronic TV transmission using a cathode ray (electron beam), which could be manipulated by electric or magnetic fields producing a much clearer image, TV's future was sealed. In 1939, W2XB began broadcasting electronic TV—it was one of the first stations to be licensed for commercial broadcasting—and has been on the air since. After World War II, W2XB became WRGB. Famous for its popular *Breadtime Stories* with Freddie Freihofer, WRGB also was home to *Answers Please, Teenage Barn,* and *TV Tournament Time.* GE and WRGB parted company in 1983 when the latter was sold to Unicom. It is now owned by the Sinclair Broadcast Group, but its heart still belongs to Schenectady.

Places to Visit in Schenectady

GE Realty Plot: East of Union College, off Nott Street, Schenectady. In 1899, Union College was looking for a way to eliminate some of its debt, and decided to sell off a 75-acre parcel of land east of the campus known as "College Woods." At the same time, GE was looking for a place to build a residential neighborhood for its scientists and executives. So in a win–win situation, Union paid off its debt with GE's $57,000 purchase of the 75 acres. The realty plot was designed by Parse and DeForrest with a plan to make a very parklike neighborhood consisting of curving roads, well-landscaped, large lots, and very grand single-family homes costing a minimum of $4,000 each (twice the going rate in 1900). Today, the realty plot covers about 90 acres and contains about 100 homes built between 1900 and 1927. Driving through the neighborhood, with its stream crossed by stone-arched bridges, and the Victorian street names such as Lenox, Wendell, and Stratford, really takes you back to a much grander time from Schenectady's past. Walking tour maps for the plot, and general info about it, are available at www.gerealtyplot.com.

Liberty Park: Corner of State Street and Washington Avenue, Schenectady, across from Schenectady County Community College. Back in the 1950s, to commemorate their 40th anniversary, the Boy Scouts of America decided to erect replicas of the Statue of Liberty across the country. There are more than 200 of these 8.5-foot copper replicas spread throughout 39 states, and New York has six of them, one located in Schenectady. The park also has the last of the historic iron signs welcoming you to Schenectady and commemorating the massacre of 1690.

Mabee Farm Historic Site: 1080 Main Street, Rotterdam Junction, 887-5073. Mabee Farm has the oldest house in the Mohawk Valley, dating back to the late 1600s. The grounds include the house, barns, the Mabee family cemetery, and beautiful gardens, all of which are open to the public. The new 13,000-square-foot George E. Franchere Education Center on the site is accessible throughout the year. The site is owned by the Schenectady County Historical Society (374-0263), which hosts numerous festivals and events there.

miSci (the Museum of Innovation and Science, formerly the Schenectady Museum): 15 Nott Terrace Heights, Schenectady, 382-7890. This is a great little museum that celebrates some of the innovations that came out of this area. It is a good museum for kids, and includes some hands-on learning. The planetarium, which was completely overhauled recently, has a full dome projection system, and has regular programming that will connect you to the stars. Dudley Observatory, with its historic library and artifacts, makes its home at the museum as well and offers a number of programs in astronomy. miSci also opens its vast archival collections on GE and some of its leading scientists to the public. Just make an appointment and be amazed.

Proctors: 432 State Street, Schenectady, 346-6204. Frederick Francis Proctor opened this theater on December 27, 1926, to rave reviews. The 2,700-seat theater was opulent and state-of-the-art. Sound was installed for the talkies in 1928, and the first public unveiling of television was here in 1930. The theater did well throughout the 1940s, but then things turned south, and eventually Proctors was closed and taken by the city for back taxes. With the theater facing a wrecking ball, in 1979 a group of concerned citizens bought Proctors from the city for $1 and revitalized it. In 2003, a $30 million expansion/renovation was begun, and today a magnificent new/old Proctors brings Broadway to upstate. The GE Theater and the smaller Upstairs@440 complete a top-notch performing-arts complex. And if that's not enough, they host the Schenectady Greenmarket here on Sundays during the winter months.

The Stockade Historic District: Bounded by Union Street on the south, the Mohawk River on the north, the Binne Kill on the west, and the railroad tracks on the east, the Stockade District is the first named historic district in New York state. It has more than 40 homes that are older than 200 years, and some date even further back than that. This is the area that came back after the massacre of 1690, which nearly wiped out Schenectady. As Schenectady and its businesses grew, the Stockade District had a number of commercial buildings mixed in with the houses. In 1819, fire destroyed more than 200 structures here, mostly commercial. The fire turned out to be a good thing for the neighborhood, because when the businesses rebuilt, they moved down to State Street to be closer to the coming Erie Canal. This left the area mostly residential. There are a number of architectural styles represented here; it's especially nice to see the old Dutch high-gabled roofs all in a row. You get a great view of these coming into Schenectady by train. The neighborhood started to decline around the 1950s, but after the first few people came in to renovate what they saw as a place with great possibilities, more followed. They formed the Stockade Association in 1962 to preserve the beauty and history of the area. The Stockade Association hosts an annual art show, usually the weekend after Labor Day. The Stockade Walkabout also is in September, usually the last Saturday. The Schenectady Historical Society makes it home in the Stockade at 32 Washington Avenue. Check out historicstockade.com for dates.

Union College: 807 Union Street, Schenectady. In 1779, people started to talk about building a place for higher education in the tri-city area.

In 1785, the Schenectady Academy, imagined by Rev. Dirck Romeyn of Schenectady's Dutch Reformed Church, became a reality. Through an interesting swirl of politics, money, and religion, this would become Union College. In 1795, Union became the first college chartered by the New York State Board of Regents, its first location being in the Stockade District. It wasn't until 1814 that it moved to its present 100-acre location off Union Street. Eliphalet Nott was president of the college from 1804 to 1866. During his long tenure, the college experienced tremendous growth and then a period of deep decline. Nott came up with a novel lottery system to raise money for the school, but his questionable practice of mixing college finances with his own brought him and the college under investigation by the New York State Senate. Although they were cleared of any wrongdoing, the scandal put Union College into a 25-year tailspin, and at its lowest point in 1888, the college lost about 75 percent of its enrollment. In 1894, Andrew Van Vranken Raymond took the helm as president. He focused on science and added a Department of Electrical Engineering and Applied Physics. He brought the brilliant (and wickedly funny) scientist Charles Steinmetz from GE to head the department. (Steinmetz gave us alternating current [AC] power.) The college was back on track.

Union has a beautiful campus, the centerpiece of which is the Nott Memorial, a 16-sided, mosaic-topped building completed in 1879. The second floor is home to the Mandeville Gallery, which is always worth visiting. US president Chester A. Arthur graduated from Union in 1848.

Vale Cemetery: 907 State Street, Schenectady, 346-0423. Vale Cemetery was founded in 1857 as part of the Rural Cemetery Movement, where smaller, in-city graveyards were relocated to large, parklike settings. Vale Cemetery and Park encompasses approximately 100 acres of trees, streams, open fields, and graves. Vale was the first cemetery in the area to have an African American graveyard, as well as a specific plot for deceased full professors of Union College. There is also Potter's Field. Although vandals have done some significant damage to many of the figures that used to watch over the graves—they are headless now and can't really do their jobs—there are still some beautiful memorials, including the "black angel" watching over the Veeder family, and "Lion" the dog who faithfully sits outside his master's vault. It is a great place to get a feel for the history of Schenectady. Check out http://valecemetery.org for upcoming tours and to see what you can do to help preserve and improve this amazing place. Vale also is the only cemetery in the area to offer green burials; you can go toxin-free into the great beyond.

The Famous Who of the Capital District

Five Fascinating Females

Invention! Sibling rivalry! Tragedy! Patriotism! And, as an added bonus, a pinch of Frisky business!!!

Hannah Lord Montague

Troy was not always the Collar City. It can thank Mrs. Montague for that nickname. Back in 1825 (or 1827, depending on your source), tired of washing and pressing her husband's entire shirt to get rid of that nasty ring around the collar, she took the bold step, and a pair of scissors, to remove the collars from the shirts and launder them separately. With ribbons attached to them, they could then be tied around his neck, making the shirt look fresh again. She remarked in a letter to a friend that her husband Orlando was not at all upset by this, and thought it quite a good idea. Word got around, and a retired minister, Rev. Ebenezer Brown, who was now busy with his dry goods store on River Street, started to manufacture detachable collars. Well, not him exactly. He got the locals to sew, clean, and press the new detachable collars for trade in his store.

Collars proved to be a big business, and everyone got into the act. Although a successful manufacturer of fine women's shoes, Orlando Montague decided to partner up with Austin Granger in 1834 to start their own collar business. They went a step further and thought, why just the collar? The dickey was born! And detachable cuffs too. With the arrival of the modern sewing machine, boom! 90 percent of collars worn around the world were from the Collar City. Maullin and Blanchard manufactured Hannah's patented collars and cuffs. George

Note: Both History Orb and Brainy History list the invention of the detachable collar as February 5, 1825. So does an article in the November 10, 1956, issue of *The New Yorker*. Arrow Shirt Co. lists 1820, local history books say 1827. Orlando is called a blacksmith, shoe manufacturer, or ironmonger. As there were 44 shoe manufacturers in Troy in the mid-1800s, we're going with that. The wittiest article on Hannah's invention is in *The Palm Beach Post* from July 12, 1925, celebrating the 100th anniversary of Mrs. Montague's grand idea. Got to love Google.

B. Cluett worked there as a clerk, eventually becoming a partner. When Maullin died, Cluett merged with Coon and Co., where Mr. Peabody worked. Cluett, Peabody and Co. was formed, and with the invention of sanforization by Sanford Cluett in 1933 to prevent shrinkage, collars were put back on shirts, and the Arrow shirt man became an icon. The last Arrow plant in Troy was closed for good in the 1980s, although most of the manufacturing had moved south decades earlier. Troy may not have the shirts anymore, but we still have the Collar City Bridge. Hannah died in 1878, and is buried in Troy's Oakwood Cemetery.

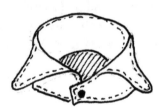

Clara Harris Rathbone

Everyone knows the horrific events of the night of April 14, 1865, at Ford's Theatre. But the devastating assassination of President Lincoln was not the only tragedy to happen that night. Young Clara Harris, daughter of New York senator Ira Harris, was in the presidential box with her fiancé, Henry Rathbone, and that night would forever change the path of their lives.

Clara Hamilton Harris was born on Sept. 4, 1834, in Albany. One of four children, Clara lost her mother when she was just 11 years old. Her father married Pauline Rathbone three years later, and brought into their family her two sons, Jared Jr. and Henry. Clara and Henry fell in love, much to their parents' dismay. A wedding was planned, but was interrupted with the outbreak of the Civil War in 1861. The Harris family moved to Washington, DC, that year (Clara's father had just been elected to the United States Senate), but kept their summer home, the Loudon Cottage, in Loudonville.

Henry became Colonel Rathbone for the Union army. The war took a huge toll on Henry; never a hardy soul, he kept having long malaria-like illnesses and yet always returned to battle. Eventually, with his stepfather's insistence and assistance, at the war's almost-end, Henry was given a desk job a few blocks from the Harris home. Meanwhile, Clara was at the top of the social ladder in Washington and was a regular visitor at the White House. When no one was available to join the Lincolns at the theater on Good Friday night, Clara and Henry were delighted to join them at the last minute. As the evening's story unfolded, Lincoln ended up slumped over in his chair with a bullet wound through his head, and Henry, having jumped up to save the president or at least capture Booth, was sliced literally to the bone by the assassin's knife. Clara was soaked in his blood. Mrs. Lincoln screamed over the sight of her husband's blood, but as Clara would write to a friend, Lincoln's wound had very little blood, and the blood she saw was all her Henry's.

Lincoln died the next morning, but Henry was sewn up, and he recovered—physically. Clara kept the bloodied dress in her closet at the family home in Loudonville, not sure what to do with it. On the one-year anniversary of Lincoln's death, while sleeping there, she was awakened by what she thought was the ghost of Lincoln laughing and rocking in his chair. So sure it was his ghost, brought to her through the dress, she had the dress sealed behind a false wall in that closet, or so the story goes.

Visitors claimed that on the anniversaries of the assassination, a gunshot could be heard in that bedroom. Mary Raymond Shipman Andrews, who made a name for herself writing "Lincoln stories," wrote a highly fictionalized, sort-of ghost story called *The White Satin Dress*, published by Scribner's in 1930. We were hoping for a cool, spooky little story, but were sadly disappointed. It was just some fluff about Lincoln's writings giving inspiration to an imaginary politician. There are no disclaimers on the book jacket, but rather, a statement that the stories are based on real incidents. But in this one, none of the names relate to anyone who ever lived other than Lincoln—and yet some people have used her writings as historical fact. So beware of some silliness out there.

Eventually, in 1867, Clara and Henry were married. They had three children, Henry Riggs, Gerald Lawrence, and Clara Pauline. Henry had never recovered from the war or from his failure to save the president. Clara often complained that the family was treated like zoo animals, with morbid curiosity seekers watching and whispering about them. Henry's mental state deteriorated, he began to drink heavily, and although well connected, could not find a suitable placement. His marriage was tense and difficult. Eventually, President Chester A. Arthur did appoint him US Consul to the Province of Hanover, Germany. The family moved to Germany hoping to find some relief for Henry's problems.

This was not to be the case. Jealous of the attention his wife paid their children, Henry purchased a gun, with which he threatened the children early on December 23, 1883. Protecting them, Clara was shot dead. Henry then stabbed himself several times but did not die. He was committed to an asylum for the criminally insane, where he lived for the next 28 years. Sadly, Clara had, a few weeks prior to her murder, written in her diary that she had never loved him more than she did then. He was eventually buried with his wife in the Engesohde Cemetery in Hanover in 1911. After Clara's murder, their children went back to the United States to be raised by their mother's brother William Harris. Local folklore has the son Henry Riggs going back to the Loudon Cottage in 1910 to break down the closet and burn the bloodied dress to remove any lingering curse it may have had on the family. Henry Riggs Rathbone became a successful lawyer in Illinois, and eventually a member of Congress, where he sponsored legislation to make Ford's Theatre a national monument. The theater was completely restored to its appearance on the night of the assassination, and Henry Riggs Rathbone was the main speaker at its dedication.

In 1952, due to lack of family interest, the bodies of Clara and Henry Rathbone were disinterred and disposed of. The Loudon Cottage still stands, although it's not quite a cottage anymore. The spirits apparently have been gone for a long time, so don't plan on any ghost hunting.

Carmela Ponselle

If you're an opera fan, you may have heard of Carmela's sister Rosa, but it was Carmela who hailed from Schenectady. Her parents were recent Italian immigrants living with relatives in Myers Alley in downtown Schenectady when Carmela Ponzillo was born, on June 7, 1887. Her mother had just turned 16. Carmela's mother confessed to her when she was older that they had desperately wanted a boy, and the disappointment of not having a son was so great that she could not even bear to look at her newborn baby girl for weeks. Luckily, she snapped out of it, and all was well.

Three years later, her brother Antonio was born during a yearlong typhoid, yes typhoid, epidemic. Carmela's Mom thought maybe it was a good time to move somewhere else. Relatives in Connecticut urged them to move to Waterbury, where Carmela's father helped out his brother in a saloon business run pretty much outside of the law. Mom was unhappy with this situation, the marriage was stressed, and when problems became too public and too embarrassing, the family left Waterbury and moved to their next home in Meriden. In 1897, Carmela's wish for a "real live baby doll" was granted with the birth of her sister Rosa. It was in Meriden that Carmela started to get noticed. By 9 she was already considered a beauty, and by 15 she was modeling for local stores. She sang in the choir, and the church organist, Miss Anna Ryan, thought Carmela had some natural talent and should consider music lessons. The family agreed, and piano and voice lessons began. By the time she was 20, Miss Ryan was sure that with Carmela's voice and looks she could make it as a singer. Meanwhile, Carmela's baby sister was listening in on every lesson, and by age 6 was learning piano as well. She would copy the songs Carmela worked on, and by age 11 or 12 was the best piano player in Meriden, with a killer voice to go with it.

Breaking with her father's wishes for her to stay at home, get married, and have babies, Carmela, on her 21st birthday, announced her desire to move to New York City and embark on a singing career. She had her mother's full support, but left for the city a few days after her birthday without even a goodbye from her father. She was set up with lodgings and a voice instructor through friends and family, and before long was singing in clubs as Miss Operetta, wowing audiences with her lovely voice and gorgeous self. She got the lead in a new musical, *The Girl from Brighton Beach*, and eventually got into vaudeville, traveling on the Keith Vaudeville Circuit. It was at this point in Carmela's life that everything changed.

As vaudeville looked for something new and different, sister acts became all the rage. Carmela had one of those, and Rosa, now 20, was old enough to join her in the city. When she brought her sister to the auditions, Carmela was politely told that Rosa—shorter and plainer than Carmela, and close to 200 pounds—was not quite the sister they were looking for. Carmela basically told them to sit down and listen, which they did, and were blown away by the voice of Rosa.

"Those Tailored Italian Girls" was one of the biggest acts to ever play vaudeville. Carmela and Rosa were making upwards of $600 a week and playing at the Palace in New York City in 1917. The sisters decided to go on strike until they were paid $1,000 a week, which was pretty much unheard of. During their time off and until their money ran out, both sisters studied nonstop so they could audition for the Metropolitan Opera Company. They thought they both had an equal shot, as sopranos were fleeing the opera at the start of World War I, and the Met was short a few. It was clear in the auditions which sister had the real talent, and it wasn't Carmela. Rosa was offered a contract to start in the fall and sing opposite Caruso.

The sisters shared their two-bedroom apartment with their voice coach, Nino Romani, and a mutual friend, Edith Prilik (who became Rosa's personal secretary), but it got so tight that they all moved to the beach in Pine Orchard, Connecticut, for the summer. Their old music teacher, Miss Ryan, also moved in. (The Ponselle sisters would take care of Miss Ryan until she died.) Rosa prepared for her roles, and Carmela spent her time on the beach sulking, realizing she was going back to vaudeville. It was this year that Rosa Ponzillo became Rosa Ponselle so as not be confused with the vaudeville Ponzillo. Carmela lived with (and lived off of) her sister once Rosa was famous. Jealous? You bet. There have always been two versions of the Ponselle story, one for the press about the girls having to save the family home and Carmela giving up everything to help her sister, but in later interviews, Rosa said it was all pretty much made up to make a good story. Carmela changed her name to Ponselle too, drawing a little more limelight her way, and eventually, in 1925, she got her contract at the Met as a mezzo-soprano after years of badgering her sister and threatening suicide if she didn't get one. She did fairly well, but her contract was allowed to lapse in 1935. Rosa considered this the time when Carmela began her decent into "dottiness."

After her tenure at the Met, Carmela taught music, then became born again, spreading the word using Rosa's money. In the 1940s she began her memoirs, tentatively titled *Romancing with the Gods, or How the Dreams of a Little Girl of Five Came True . . . Revealing the Life and Loves of the First American Mezzo-Star*. Sounded spectacular! (As far as loves, Carmela had a six-month marriage to someone from back home, and a couple of brief engagements.) She quit writing after the first six pages and put it aside. The title seemed more appropriate for her sister's life: Rosa became world famous, dined with royalty, partied with the famous in Hollywood, lived a life of luxury, and still is considered one of the best sopranos that ever lived. And American to boot. You don't have to take our word for it either. You can hear them both sing on YouTube and decide for yourself. Carmela died in 1977 after a failed operation to repair a broken hip a week after her 90th birthday. She is buried next to Rosa, who died in 1981. Giovanni Martinelli, one of the great tenors, said of Carmela, "She had the misfortune to be a sapphire mounted next to a diamond."

Catharine Van Rensselaer Schuyler

We know that the street the Schuyler Mansion still sits on is called Catherine Street with an *e*, and many sources spell her name that way, but we are using her name as it appears in letters and documents provided by her family. Catharine Van Rensselaer, the only daughter of John Van Rensselaer and Engeltie Livingston, was born November 4, 1734, at the Crailo, her family's mansion in Greenbush. The Crailo was built by her grandfather, Hendrick Van Rensselaer, who was the grandson of the first patroon, Kiliaen Van Rensselaer. Interestingly, Hendrick's wife, Catrina Van Brugh, was a granddaughter of Anneke Janse, one of Albany's first citizens, so Catharine was related to her, too. The Crailo was named for the family estate back in Holland. Most of its bricks were brought over as ballast from Holland. The original home had a special linen room, where soiled linens were kept until, *once a year*, they were sent home to Holland to be laundered. Catharine was educated at home and grew up to be a beauty in feature and spirit. Being part of the upper crust of Albany's society, she had known Philip Schuyler for a number of years before they embarked on a romantic relationship. "Kitty" and Philip married on September 17, 1755, five months before the birth of their first child, Angelica. They had 11 children through the course of their marriage, eight of whom reached maturity (see **Catharine and Philip's Children** on the next page).

Her youngest daughter, Kitty, wrote lovingly about her mother, saying she was beautiful, well educated, prudent, and a devoted wife. Basically, she thought her mom was really nice, but like most children she saw only the ordinary mom and not the extraordinary one. Catharine and Philip were married at the start of the French and Indian War, in which Philip was heavily involved. He was young, but careful, wise, and well regarded by his British superiors. In 1760 he went to England for a couple of years to settle his accounts as commissary to the British Army. Catharine was left at home in Albany, charged with overseeing the building of the Schuyler Mansion as well as raising their growing family. That's pretty impressive right there. But the American Revolution was brewing, and now General Schuyler was caught up in another war, defending the colonies against the British.

The Schuylers had another family home, more like a northern plantation, outside of Saratoga. They owned thousands of acres that included crops, a lumber mill, tenant farmers—a whole Schuyler-ville. With General Burgoyne advancing from Quebec toward what would be the pivotal Battles of Saratoga, Mrs. Schuyler took her carriage with four horses and one bodyguard from Albany to save what she could from the country estate. A few miles from their home, terrified locals implored her to turn back, as the British were approaching. The recent murder of Jane McCrea by British allies had everyone in fear. Mrs. Schuyler merely replied, "The general's wife must not be afraid." She made it to the house, then received word from her husband to burn the crops and implore the tenants to do the same; the British were almost on their doorstep. Catharine went to the fields and burned them down by her own hand. She sent her horses on to the patriot army and traveled back to Albany on an oxen-drawn sled.

In 1852, this event was immortalized in a painting by Emanuel Leutze (who also painted *Washington Crossing the Delaware*), called *Mrs. Schuyler Burning Her Wheat Fields on the Approach of the British*. This painting is owned by the Los Angeles County Museum of Art, and depending on when you visit, it may or may not be on display. (Really? LA? Shouldn't it be here?) Burgoyne made it to the Saratoga house and burned it down along with everything else. He felt kind of bad about this after his surrender, as he was "imprisoned" at the Schuyler Mansion in Albany and treated with grace and kindness by the entire Schuyler family. He got to invite his wife and family over, who were also treated as old friends rather than people who had *burned down their home and tried to kill them*. After the war and a few more children, Catharine lived out the remainder of her life at the Schuyler Mansion. She died in 1803.

Catharine and Philip's Children

Angelica, born in 1756 and christened Engeltie, eloped with John Barker Church, and depending on sources, had two to nine children. We can find clear references to two, Philip and Catharine. She died in 1814.

Elizabeth, born in 1757, married Alexander Hamilton and had eight children with him. Their eldest, the first of their two Philips, died in a duel three years before his father's death in the infamous duel with Aaron Burr. After Hamilton's death, Elizabeth lived another 50 years and died at 97 in 1854.

Margarita, born in 1758, married the second-to-last patroon, Stephen Van Rensselaer. She had two children with him. She predeceased Van Rensselaer, who remarried within a few years. Stephen was the founder of what would become RPI.

John Bradstreet, born in 1763, was named for Colonel Bradstreet, a close friend and frequent guest at the Schuyler home. "Johnny" married Elizabeth Van Rensselaer, but died at 30. His father had given him the Saratoga estate to manage, but after his death he left this property to John's son Philip.

Philip Jeremiah, born in 1768. His father wrote to his daughter Angelica about his disappointment in Philip and his lack of serious study. Philip married Sarah Rutsen, an heiress of Wilhemus Beekman, who owned most of Dutchess County. They lived near Rhinebeck, and Philip served in the US House of Representatives. After Sarah's death, he married Mary Ann Sawyer. Philip died in 1835.

Rensselaer, born in 1773, married Elizabeth Ten Broeck. They had no children.

Cornelia, born in 1776. Her father strongly objected to her choice in suitors, so like her sister, she eloped, marrying a New Jerseyan named Washington Morton in Massachusetts. The father-daughter rift lasted for years, but she was forgiven before Philip died, leaving her an equal share in his estate. She had five children, but died young at 32 in 1808.

Note: There are a couple of interesting reads if you really enjoy Albany history. One is *A Godchild of Washington*, written by Catharine's great granddaughter Katharine Schuyler Baxter in 1897. It includes a lot of previously unpublished family letters, and intimate bios of Albany's who's who from the beginning, as well as a ton of beautiful etchings and photographs you probably won't find anywhere else. Another is *Memoirs of an American Lady* by Scottish author and poet Anne Grant, written in 1808. The American lady is Catalina Schuyler, a beloved aunt of General Schuyler.

Our only issue with the latter is that it is written in a time when *s*'s are written like *f*s. Fo if that doefn't drive you crazy, the ftory if really quite entertaining. You can sometimes snag an original copy of these on eBay. The originals are much better than the reprinted versions if you want clarity on the images.

Catharine Van Rensselaer, born in 1781, was George Washington's goddaughter and, apparently, her father's favorite. She was called "Kitty" just like her mom. Catharine married Samuel B. Malcolm and had two children with him. They moved to Utica, but before Malcolm's death in 1817, they returned to Albany. Kitty married James Cochran in 1822, and in 1825, Kitty, John, and her two children moved to Oswego. She died in 1857.

Mame Faye

Before anyone "hiked the Appalachian Trail," at the beginning of the last century, they would take "a weekend trip to Troy." Mame Faye was one of the legendary madames of Troy's red-light district on 6th Avenue for 40 years. Mame Faye (Fay) was born Mary Alice Fahey in 1866 to Thomas Fahey and Margaret McNamara. She had a sister Martha, and a brother Thomas, who was killed by a D&H train in 1896. Her sister married and lived in Troy. Mame had a very short-lived marriage to someone named Bonter; in one census she was Mrs. Bonter, but by the next she was Mary Bonter, single or widowed. Also, by the second census, she had moved in with her sister and brother-in-law Michael Myers.

She also had decided on a new career path. Although arrested for disorderly conduct in 1904, she was not dissuaded by this and bought her first bordello in 1906 at 1725 6th Avenue. It was located in the middle of a line of row houses (all red-light establishments), across from Union Station and at the bottom of the approach to RPI. The location really couldn't have been better. The police station was three doors down, and officers worked as bouncers on their nights off. Yes, this was all illegal, but early on the Victorians saw these establishments as necessary evils rather than great social ills, as they came to be known by the '40s. During Prohibition, Troy's location on the Hudson, just off the Erie and Champlain Canals, made it an easy place to offload barrels of Canadian alcohol, adding to the appeal of 6th Avenue. The brothel owners made no secret of their businesses, and ran ads for "Troy's Famous Red Light District Known Coast to Coast Satisfaction Guaranteed—$2.00." Mame Fay's Notchery, as well as Lottie Denver's Cupcake Revue and Mildred Hamilton's Sandwich Shoppe, all were prominently advertised.

Mame would go looking for new employees in the local lunch shops. Legend has it that Mame Faye or another madam, when asking the girls what they were making in a local factory, she would quip, "Honey, don't you know you're sittin' on a million?" Mame would offer them $100 a week, a large jump over their usual $15 to $18 a week. Business was great for almost 40 years, and then, as social mores changed and pressure from local politicians increased, Mame, at 75, decided to close up shop and retire. She lived with her nephew Thomas Myers in Troy, leaving her quite considerable estate to him when she died two years

> **Note:** In 2008, a short documentary called *Sittin' on a Million* was released by local filmmakers Penny Lane and Annmarie Lanesey. The short clips we've been able to see on various online sites include some very sweet recollections of an apparently very special lady.

later in 1943. She is buried in St. Joseph's Cemetery. She had set aside $2,500 for a headstone, which she finally got in 2006.

As often is the case with urban renewal, in 1952, Troy's city fathers decided to knock down all of 6th Avenue, including the magnificent Union Station. This "improvement" destroyed about a third of Troy's historic downtown.

Four Famous Phils of Albany

Philip Livingston

Philip Livingston was born on January 15, 1716, to one of Albany's prominent (or shall we say rich and powerful) families. His family home was at the corner of State and North Pearl streets (a Starbucks sits in its place now; there is a plaque on the outside wall to tell you about the Livingston home). On this site in the 1730s, young Philip planted an elm tree that stood on this corner until it was taken down on June 15, 1877. The tree became a landmark, and the corner was known as Elm Tree Corner for years after the tree was gone. It also was known as Hanging Elm Tree Corner, and many were hanged until dead from the tree's limbs, including two young slaves (12- and 14-year-old girls) accused of setting the fire of 1793 that destroyed more than 60 buildings on Broadway, including the first Ten Broeck mansion. A third slave implicated in the scheme to start the fire, a young man named Pomp, was hanged a few months later in the same spot.

Livingston graduated from Yale in 1737 (as did most of his family; his father had donated a *lot* of money to the school.) When his father died, being the fourth son, Philip was not heir to his father's considerable estate. He moved to New York City, where he became a very successful merchant. He married Christina Ten Broeck, with whom he had nine children. He bought up a lot of what became Brooklyn Heights, and built his mansion there; his carriage road is now Livingston Street. Philip understood the importance of higher education, and was one of the founders of King's College, later Columbia.

Livingston became more and more involved in the politics of the day, and we are talking American Revolution politics of the day. He had been a delegate to the Albany Congress in 1754, as well as an alderman in New York City. In 1765 he attended the Stamp Act Congress, which basically wrote the first "Dear John" letter to England—sort of the prelude to the Declaration of Independence. His fight for independence was already in full swing in the 1770s, as he helped gather support and raise money for an army. He was a delegate to the Continental Congress in 1775 and one of the signers of the Declaration of Independence in 1776. (His younger brother William, who had moved to New Jersey and became its first elected governor, was a signer of the US Constitution.)

Philip was elected to the New York State Senate in 1777, and continued to work with the Continental Congress, but his health was rapidly failing. He realized his time would be short, and said goodbye to his family in Kingston (they had moved there from New York City to escape the British Army) and his friends and family in Albany. In May 1978, he went to York, Pennsylvania, to join the congress, but died the next month. The entire congress attended his funeral as one body and observed a one-month period of mourning. Livingston is buried in York, Pennsylvania.

Philip Schuyler

Philip Schuyler was born on November 11, 1733, to one of the wealthiest families in Albany. Schuylerville, Schuyler Flats, Schuyler Bakery, you know the name. He married Catharine Van Rensselaer in September 1755, just five months before the birth of their first daughter, Angelica. Human gestation apparently was much shorter in colonial times. They were a devoted couple, producing 11 children, eight of whom survived. He referred to Catharine as "My Dear Love" in all of his letters.

During the French and Indian War (1755–1760), Schuyler commanded a company in New York for the British Army. At war's end, on a trip to finish up paperwork for the British, the captain of the ship died, and Schuyler took over, navigating the ship through severe gales, a capture by French mercenaries, and recapture by British forces. He eventually brought the ship safely into London's harbor.

After the war, he busied himself raising his family and running a very large estate left to him by his father. As the colonies were becoming more and more disgruntled with British rule, Schuyler, much like Livingston, took up the cause. He was one of four major generals appointed under Washington. Schuyler's job was to plan and implement an attack against Canada. Because of his poor health (he suffered from gout and was in chronic pain), he turned over this plan to Gen. Richard Montgomery. However, Schuyler had been too slow executing his plan, and the attack failed. In 1777, British General John Burgoyne managed to win the northern stronghold of Fort Ticonderoga due to perceived incompetence on Schuyler's part. Schuyler demanded a court martial to clear his name. He was acquitted of any wrongdoing, but resigned his post soon thereafter. In the 1821 painting *Surrender of General Burgoyne* by John Trumbull, which depicts Burgoyne's surrender after the second battle of Saratoga on October 17, 1777, you can see the image of Philip Schuyler, fifth from the right, standing with the other generals but himself clad in his street clothes rather than his general's uniform.

After the Revolutionary War, Schuyler became involved in local politics and served as a New York State senator for 13 years. He was considered the father of our canal system, and was president of both the Northern and Western Canal Companies in 1792. He spent 10 years working, sketching and executing plans for a canal system west of Schenectady to Little Falls and north to Lake Champlain. The Erie Canal was finally finished and opened in October 1825 through the perseverance of Governor DeWitt Clinton. In his final years, Schuyler dedicated himself to developing a new system of surveying, and spent many hours discussing the subject with his dear friend and mathematician Dr. David Rittenhouse of Philadelphia. He apparently sent his finished work to his friend in Philadelphia, but that letter never arrived, leaving it a mystery. He served as a US senator for one term before losing his seat to Aaron Burr. (Yes, the Aaron Burr who killed Schuyler's son-in-law, Alexander Hamilton.) Burr won the seat in the Senate due to the efforts of the Livingston and Clinton families. (And yes, again, that Livingston family.) Schuyler won the seat back in 1797 with the help of Hamilton. The grudge match between Burr and Hamilton continued until Burr killed Hamilton in a duel in 1804. Schuyler died in November 1804, a few months after the death of his beloved wife Catharine and his beloved son-in-law Hamilton.

Schuyler left behind a remarkable legacy (besides everything with his name on it). He was considered a great friend of the Six Nations, a devoted husband and father, a visionary, a war hero, and a public servant. He always studied, and encouraged all of his children to as well. (He started to study German in his last years just so he could read certain books on surveying techniques that had yet to be translated). His letters, especially to his daughter Angelica, covered broad and complex discussions on politics and religion.

In 1925, a statue of Philip Schuyler by J. Massey Rhind was erected in front of Albany City Hall.

Philip Hooker

You may not be familiar with the name, but Philip Hooker was one of Albany's foremost architects in the late 1700s. Hooker was born October 28, 1766, in Rutland, Massachusetts. His parents, Samuel and Rachel, were married a few months earlier in July. (Again, the gestation period was much shorter back then.) Samuel was a carpenter and a builder, and it was from his father that Philip learned the trade. Philip and his family moved to Albany when he was six years old, and he stayed here until his death in 1836.

Hooker was very involved in local government, and served as Albany's assessor seven times, as well as city superintendent and city surveyor. He began designing and building a lot of Albany's buildings at this time, not so much because he was a brilliant architect but because he was known and trusted. Up to this point, Albany's architecture remained much more medieval than in the other New England states. Although all of New England started out with a more ancient look, by the later 17th century, the style was changing east of Albany. The Dutch never really embraced the Renaissance style of architecture, whereas the British loved it and passed it on to their colonies. Visitors called the Albany style "Dutch Gothic," and the old gabled roofs and pigs wandering the streets led people to insult the city by calling it "more Dutch than decent."

It may well have had a medieval look to it, but by the Revolutionary War and later, Albany became one very important place of power and industry. The newly arriving residents really wanted a new look. Enter Philip Hooker.

Hooker did not have the advantage of growing up near large cities or traveling to Europe to develop his skills. He learned by copying from other architects in New England, and reading architecture books from England. He was called unsophisticated, but his buildings were clean and not overly ornamented, and were considered unmistakably American.

By 1833, after Hooker's heyday as an architect, if you looked around Albany, you saw the buildings he designed everywhere: five churches; all three banks in town; both schools, including Albany Academy; City Hall; the state capitol; three downtown markets; the Proctor Leland and Pearl Street theaters; and numerous private homes. There was, literally, a Hooker on every corner in Albany, and his buildings gave the city a more stately appearance.

Hooker was married twice but had no children. He is buried with his first wife in the Albany Rural Cemetery. Almost every Hooker building has been demolished, destroyed by fire, or remodeled beyond recognition, but there are still a few left in town, including First Church on North Pearl, the original Albany Academy, which is now the administration building of the City School District of Albany, and a once-private mansion built for Samuel Hill, which is now the Fort Orange Club at 110 Washington Avenue. In Troy, the Hart-Cluett mansion, at 59 2nd Street, also is credited to Hooker.

The definitive book on Hooker is by Edward W. Root. Written in 1929, *Philip Hooker* is a complete overview of his buildings with amazing photographs to complement the descriptions. The author apologizes for the lack of personal accounts of the man, as by 1929 any acquaintances or family of Hooker were gone.

Philip Sheridan

Did you ever wonder who that guy was on the horse in front of the state capitol? A very impressive looking man on a very impressive looking horse. The man was General Philip Sheridan, and the horse was named Rienzi. The jet-black horse was a 16-hand Morgan (that's a pretty tall horse); Sheridan on the other hand was five feet five in his boots. Nicknamed "Little Phil," he was said to have had to shimmy up his saber to get up into his saddle. Abraham Lincoln said Sheridan had such long arms that if his ankles itched he could scratch them without stooping. Hooray for artistic license!

Sheridan was born on March 6, 1831, some say in Albany, others Ohio, and some say on the boat coming over from Ireland (at 17, Sheridan decided it was Albany). When Governor Martin Glynn decided he wanted an Irishman in front of the capitol, Philip Sheridan was chosen. He did grow up in Ohio, and eventually was admitted to West Point, where it took him five years to graduate. Apparently, he was held back for fighting with another cadet. Although not an impressive student, he became an outstanding commander, rapidly rising to major general during the Civil War. On October 19, 1864, at the crucial battle of Cedar Creek in Virginia's Shenandoah Valley, Sheridan, riding on top of the magnificent Rienzi, rallied his demoralized and panicked troops to victory. The famous ride was immortalized in Thomas Read's poem "Sheridan's Ride," which was published everywhere in the North to promote the Union war effort.

Rienzi saw 19 battles and was wounded several times. When the horse died at a pretty good age at his master's home, Sheridan had him stuffed and put on display in the first US Army Museum in Manhattan, which was destroyed by fire in 1922. Rienzi, however, was saved and escorted to the Smithsonian Museum, where you can see him today, encased in glass in the Hall of Armed Forces History.

Sheridan is hated by Virginians because he was responsible for burning Virginia down to ensure the Union win in the Shenandoah Valley. In 1865, he pursued General Robert E. Lee and was instrumental in Lee's forced surrender at Appomattox. After the Civil War, Sheridan served in the Department of the Missouri, where his job was to crush the Plains Indians. He was accused of genocide and racism, and given credit for the quote "the only good Indians I ever saw were dead." He steadfastly denied saying this.

Sheridan bore much responsibility for the near-extinction of the American bison. As the herds were being slaughtered, in 1875, the Texas Legislature considered a bill to protect the dwindling bison population. Sheridan stepped in, commending the buffalo hunters for destroying the main support of the culture and existence of the Plains tribes. Between 1868 and 1881, the bones of nearly 700,000 slaughtered bison were scavenged off the plains to be used in refining sugar and assorted bric-a-brac. Martin S. Garretson, in his 1938 book *The American Bison*, called the slaughter "wasteful butchery, inspired by greed."

In 1875, Sheridan married Irene Rucker, with whom he had four children. After a series of heart attacks, he died on August 5, 1888. After his death, his wife never remarried and said she would rather be the widow of Phil Sheridan than the wife of any living man. The statue of Sheridan and Rienzi was unveiled in front of the New York State Capitol in October 1916. In a letter to Governor Charles S. Whitman a year earlier, Mrs. Sheridan protested that the planned memorial statue "did not bear any resemblance to her husband"; however, her objection was overruled by committee.

Three Thrilling Henrys

Henry Hudson

Henry Hudson spent only a few days here in September 1609 while he was sulking over not finding the Northwest Passage to Asia via our beautiful river. He never even came back for a visit, but we credit him with starting the ball rolling as far as Albany's future was concerned. If it weren't for Henry, we could have ended up French!

As is often the case, we didn't care much about who Hudson was until after he became famous for his journey, in which he sailed up the Hudson River on the Half Moon. He vanished two years later, and so we don't know a whole lot about him. There isn't even an actual likeness of him, just drawings made from recollections well after his death.

Most scholars go along with 1570 as his year of birth, and possibly September 12 being his actual birthday. It is generally assumed that he got in a lot of sailing experience as a young man, but the only recorded trips are the biggies in which he was searching for the Northeast or Northwest passages to get to the silks and spices of Asia for various trading companies. His grandfather had a controlling share in the Muscovy Company, so his first two important trips on his quest to sail over the North Pole were for his grandfather's company (in 1607 and 1608). Both of these voyages ended in defeat for Henry as ice blocked his route and he had to return home. The trip that put Albany on the map was the voyage of 1609.

Henry was a man on a mission at this point, and was bent on finding that Northwest Passage. In January 1609, he signed a contract with the Dutch East India Company, which guaranteed him payment of 800 guilders to make the trip, and his wife 200 guilders if he didn't make it back alive. In turn, he promised to deliver to the company all of the information he would gather, including all of his logs, with nothing held back. Not widely known is that two ships—the Half Moon and the Good Hope—were sent out together on that March 25, heading first north and then west. Again, Hudson was stopped by ice.

Although he had been ordered to return to Holland if unsuccessful, Henry decided, what the heck, I've got the keys to the boat and I'm heading west! The Good Hope said "no way" and returned home. Hudson believed he would locate the Northwest Passage in America, following the Grande Rive (named by Verrazano in 1524 while working for the French, who were actually the first Europeans to be trading here, in the 1500s) over the top of the world. Eventually this river would be called the Hudson, but not until late in the 1800s. Prior to that, it was widely known as the North River.

What is interesting here is that Hudson's logs for 1607, 1608, and 1610–1611 all have been reprinted, but the one that would mean the most to Albany was sold at auction in 1821 with other papers from the Dutch East India Company, and basically has vanished. Our information about that trip is mostly taken from the journal of Robert Juet. Hudson and Juet disliked each other, but Hudson hired him three times, twice as mate. Although Juet was an expert sailor, some referred to him as Hudson's evil genius. On the Half Moon voyage, a Dutch sailor actually was the first mate.

Sadly for Hudson, the big river provided no outlet to Asia. In fact, shallow water forced him to stop his trip at Albany. He anchored here for four days, trading with the locals, before heading back to Europe. He thought he would stop off in England to visit the family before returning to Amsterdam; arriving in Dartmouth on November 7, 1609, Hudson was promptly arrested for treason (sailing under another country's flag), and the Half Moon and its Dutch crew sailed back to Amsterdam with Hudson's logs and booty.

Not one to give up, Hudson, once released from his "arrest," tried one last time to find the elusive passage, this time sailing for the British East India Company with the ship Discovery. Although he arrived in Hudson Bay in August 1610, Hudson spent too many months mapping the shores, and ended up stuck in the ice for the winter. The crew was pretty unhappy at this point, including first mate Juet. When the ice finally melted the following June, Juet instigated a mutiny and dumped Hudson, his son John, and seven of his loyal crew into a small boat and left them to die in the open waters of Hudson Bay; presumably they did. However, a 150-pound rock was found in 1959 by a road crew near Chalk River, Ontario (south of Hudson Bay, but reachable by river routes), which had carved into it "HH 1612 CAPTIVE." So who really knows for sure?

Hudson left behind a wife and two sons. His wife went on to become a wealthy woman, working for the East India Company.

Here is one of our secret family recipes. This one is from our Hungarian gypsy aunt, who was one of the best bakers we knew.

Half Moon Cookies

Cream:
2 sticks of butter
¾ cup of sugar
2 teaspoons of vanilla
1 tablespoon of water

Add:
½ teaspoon of salt
2 cups of flour
6 ounces of finely chopped pecans

When this is all blended, shape into small crescents (or half moons) and place on an ungreased cookie sheet. Bake at 350 degrees for about 20 minutes until slightly golden. When cool enough to handle, put them in a bag with ¼ cup confectioner's sugar and shake gently until coated. Refrigerate them so this sticks, and then coat them again, this time with ½ cup confectioner's sugar.

You good cooks out there will notice there is no leavening in these cookies, and yes, that is correct.

Henry Hobson Richardson

We really like Henry Hobson Richardson. He is known as the *first* American architect. Together with Louis Sullivan and Frank Lloyd

Wright, Richardson completes the trinity of American architecture. Albany is home to two of his glorious buildings. He was one of the last architects working on the capitol, and then he designed Albany City Hall across the street. In Troy, the Gardner Earl Chapel was built in the Richardsonian Romanesque style (an actual architectural type named for him) two years after Richardson's death.

Richardson was born September 29, 1838, in Louisiana. He was one of four children. He was raised in New Orleans and was called "Fez" by his family and friends. At age 18 he went off to Harvard, and from there, to the Ecole des Beaux-Arts in France. He was only the second American to be accepted to study there. Upon returning home, he married Julia Gorham Hayden, the sister of a Harvard classmate, and had six children. He began his career immediately with a commission to build the Church of the Unity in Massachusetts in 1866.

Richardson wasn't interested in designing buildings in the popular Victorian Gothic styles, but took his inspiration from the medieval period. He was so into the 11th century that he often roamed around in monks' robes. You can Google his image and see a number of photographs of him wearing a monk's outfit. His style reflected the man himself. It was massive and dramatic. Richardson was well over six feet tall and weighed more than 300 pounds. He died on April 27, 1886, at age 48 from complications of Bright's disease (a kidney disorder). Although his design career was cut short, of 10 buildings voted the most successful examples of architectural design in the country in 1885, five were designed by Richardson, and two of those five are in Albany.

The first appearance of his distinctive Romanesque style was seen in the Buffalo State Asylum in 1869, followed by Boston's Trinity Church in 1872. In Albany, when the first architect (Thomas Fuller) for the New York State Capitol building was fired, Richardson, Leoplold Eidlitz, and Fredrick Law Olmsted drew up new plans with a more Renaissance/

Romanesque style. Fuller completed the first floor from 1867 to 1875, Richardson and Eidlitz the second two floors between 1875 and 1883, and ultimately, when Governor Grover Cleveland got antsy about a completion date, he fired Richardson and Eidlitz and hired Isaac Perry to complete the project, but Richardson and Eidlitz continued to consult and influence the outcome. The Million Dollar Staircase was designed by Richardson.

When the old City Hall burned down in 1880, Richardson was commissioned to build the new one. Learning from the mistakes made in funding the capitol, city fathers enforced a strict budget in constructing the new city hall. With money tight, Richardson focused on the exterior design. The massive stone, banded arched doors and windows, fanciful carvings (by the same stonecutters who worked on the capitol), and tower make this one of the things Albany did right. The tower was designed to hold the city's archives, but was repurposed as a carillon in 1927. The building's exterior was finished in 1883, but the interior was not quite done until 1917. Richardson had hoped to continue his transformation of Albany with a commission for the Cathedral of All Saints, but it was given to someone else, leaving him pretty miffed. His last project, largely designed and completed by his firm, was the Grange Sard House at 397 State Street, Albany. Although he did not design anything else for Albany, other buildings were built in his style, notably the Albany Armory and the Gardner Earl Memorial Chapel and Crematorium in Troy.

H. H. Richardson preferred designing the more monumental structures, but did design a number of libraries, train stations, and private residences. The Glessner House in Chicago is the most famous, but our favorite was Lululaund. Richardson met artist Hubert von Herkomer on one of the artist's trips to America. In exchange for a very cool portrait, Richardson drew sketches for a four-story Romanesque castle, which von Herkomer had built in England between 1886 and 1894. The house was named for his deceased wife, Lulu. Even though von Herkomer died in 1914, right before World War I, the house ended up being dismantled, in part because of anti-German sentiment, but also because it presented a great target for enemy bombers. Only the facade was preserved and put to use as the door on a British Legion Hall.

Richardson considered the Marshall Field Wholesale Store he designed in Chicago, one of his last, to be one of his most significant works. It was demolished in 1930 to put up a parking lot.

Henry Johnson

Nearly 100 years late, Henry Johnson, who lived most of his adult life in Albany, finally was awarded the Medal of Honor in May 2015. The award is given by the president to those who have performed personal acts of valor above and beyond the call of duty.

Johnson's life history is a short story. Not even his name is a certainty. He went by Henry Lincoln Johnson, but was buried at Arlington National Cemetery as William Henry Johnson. (His wife was quoted as calling him "Bill" in newspapers after the war, so it could be either). He was born in 1891 in a post-Reconstruction, Jim Crow-controlled North Carolina. As a teen, he moved to Albany, where he worked various jobs, ending up as a porter at Albany's Union Station. He married, and may have had three children.

In April 1917, the United States declared war on Germany. In June, Henry Johnson, wanting to fight for his country, traveled to Brooklyn to join the only African-American regiment, the old 15th, later to become the 369th Infantry Regiment of the US Army, aka the Harlem Hellfighters. In 1913, our first Southern president, Woodrow Wilson, segregated not only federal workplaces but the military as well, believing that an African American could not be trained as a fighting soldier.

The old 15th was predominantly black except for the colonels and majors, which the state mandated to be white. Luckily, Johnson's regiment was assigned a Colonel William Hayward, who believed that with training and discipline every regiment would be equal. Johnson's regiment was sent to the South (the South!) for training, but due to fights with the white regiments, they were sent back north and quickly dispatched to France with little or no training. Once there, they were given the tasks of digging latrines and hauling supplies. Not likely to see battle with the US Army, the 369th was detailed to the French, who were desperate for any men willing to fight. The night of May 13, 1918, is the one day of Henry's life that is verifiable and completely extraordinary.

Johnson and Neadom Roberts (a 17-year-old bellhop from Trenton, New Jersey) were on sentry duty in the Argonne woods when they heard German soldiers breaking into their camp to capture soldiers. To protect their other men, Johnson and Roberts went on the attack. Grenades and gunfire inflicted severe physical damage to both; Roberts was down, but Johnson, even with wounds to his body and a destroyed foot, running on adrenalin, fired on the Germans until his gun locked and then used it as a battering ram on the Germans that surrounded him. As he saw the Germans trying to haul off Roberts, he followed them and with his bolo knife took down two of them. Critically injured, Johnson was still able to get up and fight. He continued to throw grenades at the retreating Germans.

When morning came, Johnson had 21 wounds, but he, Roberts, and the rest of the men were alive. The commissioner of the regiment would later write to Mrs. Johnson that there were as many as 12 German casualties. Major Arthur Little wrote a full account of the battle the next morning, which was published in his book *From Harlem to the Rhine*. Johnson was awarded France's highest honor, the Croix de Guerre with Gold Palm. Johnson became famous overnight. Private Johnson became

Sergeant Johnson. "Black Death" returned to New York City to a ticker-tape parade; they were the new faces of recruiting and bond posters. "The Battle of Henry Johnson" was used to illustrate the strength and dedication of all soldiers. Promises were made and quickly forgotten. No medals were to be had.

Henry Johnson had a very short-lived speaking career after he returned. He focused on the inequities he faced in the army. He said that had he been white, he would have become governor of the state. Instead, they arrested him for wearing his uniform past its expiration date. He tried to return to work, but his injuries made that impossible. His marriage failed, he began to drink, and he died in 1929.

Johnson remained largely forgotten until family and friends decided it was time to right the wrongs of the US Army and celebrate a local hero. The late John Howe of Albany, a Vietnam War veteran, together with the support of local veterans and Johnson's family, worked tirelessly from the 1970s to do this. In 1991, Henry Johnson Boulevard was named in his honor. In 1997, he was awarded the Purple Heart for injuries sustained in battle. Once his grave was found at Arlington in 2001, the Distinguished Service Cross was awarded, in 2003, for extraordinary heroism. There are statues in Arbor Hill and Washington Park remembering him. And finally, the Medal of Honor. A really good account taken from Major Little's book of Henry's battle is in another old book by Theodore Roosevelt Jr. called *Rank and File* (1928). It is well worth reading the full account of the battle. In the book, Roosevelt calls Henry Johnson one of the top five American heroes of World War I.

One surprising outcome of the fight for the Medal of Honor was the discovery that Herman Johnson, a World War II Tuskegee Airman who believed Henry was his father and fought for his recognitions, was not a blood relative, according to birth certificates. He and his daughter honored him as their family, and Henry treated Herman as his son. That's still family.

Two Super Stephens

Stephen Myers

Not many people in Albany are aware of the part the city played in the Underground Railroad, and even fewer are familiar with Stephen Myers, a freed slave, who was one of the main activists in this area.

Stephen Myers was born a slave in Rensselaer County in 1800. He was freed at 18 and worked a number of jobs in the upstate region. In 1827 he married Harriet Johnson. Her family owned a sloop (*Miriam*) for transporting goods up and down the river. In the 1830s, Stephen and Harriet began transporting more than just cargo in their efforts to aid those on the Underground Railroad. Their stop on the secret network was considered to be one of the most effective, helping possibly thousands to escape slavery. As an outspoken proponent of the antislavery movement along with his wife, Myers published a newspaper in the early 1940s called *The Northern Star and Freeman's Advocate*.

Living on the Hudson gave Myers access to contacts along the river all the way to New York City. He held meetings at his house, and aided great numbers of fleeing slaves by giving them a safe house and assistance in getting to Canada. He became president of the New York State Suffrage Association, which tried to have the $250 property requirement for black citizens eliminated. During this time, Myers also became a trustee of the Florence Farming and Lumber Association, which planned a community in Oneida where black citizens could settle and make a living. The community failed for a number of reasons, but mostly because of the Fugitive Slave Act of 1850, which required the return of captured slaves to their previous owners. Fearful of being returned to a life they had struggled greatly to escape, most preferred the freedom of Canada.

What's amazing is that Harriet and Stephen Myers' house, built in 1847 by Harriet's father John Johnson, is still standing at 194 Livingston Street (formerly Lumber Street). This historic site was saved by Mary Liz and Paul Stewart, who have invested a number of years researching and teaching about the history of the UR in Albany. After a very tedious restoration process, it looks like the house is almost there. They give walking tours on the subject (Underground Railroad History Project, 432-4432) during the warm months.

The Myerses worked for the cause between 1830 and the 1850s. Harriet died in 1865, and Stephen died on February 13, 1870, in Albany. Look for his house to open as a living museum in the future. To help, you can contact the Stewarts at the Underground Railroad History Project.

Stephen Van Rensselaer III

This Stephen, not number II or IV, definitely deserves a special hooray in the history of this area. Not because he was a patroon, which could be a bad thing, but because he was the last patroon, and actually was called "The Good Patroon."

Stephen III was born in New York City in 1764, but grew up here in the Van Rensselaer Manor House. His mother was a Livingston, his uncle was Abraham Ten Broeck, and when his father died, his mother married Domine Westerlo. You probably recognize these names. Stephen graduated from Harvard at age 18 (after his education at Princeton was interrupted by those pesky British) and a year later, on June 6, 1783, when he was just 19, he eloped with Margarita, one of the Schuyler daughters. He and Margarita had three children. After her death in 1801, he married the daughter of New Jersey's governor, Cornelia Paterson, with whom he had another 10 children.

When Stephen was 21 years old, he took control of the family estate, or patroonship. In the early days of Albany's development, the Dutch wanted as many warm bodies here as possible to protect their trade interests against any other group of immigrants. They initiated a patroon system, which was basically a feudal system, where they would give away large tracts of land to a patroon for bringing over 50 settlers. Kiliaen Van Rensselaer knew a good thing when he saw it and took full advantage of this deal. Although he never personally set foot here, his heirs were plentiful and everywhere. When the English took over, they respected this arrangement and let the patroons live on. They changed the terminology slightly, and the patroons became landlords, charging their tenants rent and taxes on the land they worked. After the American Revolution, you can imagine how the hard-working tenants began to feel about this system.

Stephen III, having inherited a huge amount of land and seeing no easy way to take care of it, concocted a scheme to entice farmers to settle on his land. He offered 120 acres, free for seven years, to anyone who would clear and maintain the land. They would receive a lease at the end of the seven years, but could not see that lease until the seven years was up. After the "free" period was over, the farmers were shocked to find that they weren't given title to the land but instead were expected to pay rent and taxes, and supply free labor to the patroon (Stephen III) without having any rights to the water, timber, or anything else that might be on their land. This marked the beginning of the end.

Stephen III knew it would be hard to collect the rent so, in large part, he let it slide, making him "The Good Patroon." This, however, backfired on his son, Stephen IV who, upon his father's death in 1839, had to pay all of his father's debts ($400,000) and was directed to use back rents to do so. Sure, like that was going to work.

The Anti-Rent Wars began in upstate New York almost immediately and lasted until 1846. This was a hard-fought battle between the farmers and law enforcement. The militia was called in to quell the insurrection when a deputy sheriff was killed in 1845. The resistance turned to politics, and elected a new governor, John Young, who pushed the state to amend its constitution and to outlaw long-term leases.

About 15 years before his death, Stephen III decided it was time for a learning institute "for the purpose of instructing persons, who may choose to apply themselves, in the application of science to the common purposes of life." And so, in 1824, the Rensselaer School got its start. It would become the Rensselaer Institute 10 years later (RPI today), and in 1835, eight women graduated, completing a special mathematics course. Stephen III served his state out of a sense of duty, working in the Assembly and Senate, and as lieutenant governor of New York, pushing for unpopular reforms like extended suffrage. He served on the Canal Commission from 1816 to 1839. RPI actually had a summer session in 1830 on the "Rensselaer School Flotilla" on the Erie Canal. Van Rensselaer died in 1839 and was buried in the family plot, but was moved to Albany Rural Cemetery when the manor was moved to Williams College (to be used as a frat house, but demolished in 1973) and everybody had to move—dead or alive.

One Unbelievable Uncle Sam

In 1961, by a formal resolution, Congress decided to make it very clear that Uncle Sam was indeed based on the real live person that was Samuel Wilson of Troy. Sam Wilson was born in what became Arlington, Massachusetts, on September 13, 1766, one of 13 children born to Edward and Lucy Wilson. (Arlington has a lovely monument to mark the birthplace of its native son, "Uncle Sam.") The family moved to New Hampshire when Sam was a teenager. He enlisted in the revolutionary army, where his duties were caring for cattle and slaughtering and packaging meat. In 1789, Samuel and his older brother Ebenezer decided to move to Vanderheyden, New York, to seek their fortunes. They walked! By the time they got there it had changed its name to Troy.

The brothers' first joint venture was a brickmaking firm. It was very successful, but four years later, they opened up the E. and S. Wilson meatpacking business. This too became very profitable and became their primary business (they still kept the brickyard, though). Sam married Betsy Mann of New Hampshire in 1797. As the meatpacking business grew to include their own docks, sloops, and a farm for pasturing (now Prospect Park), numerous relatives of the Wilson and Mann clans moved to Troy to help in the family business. "Uncle Sam" was loved by his family and the city of Troy. Always civic minded, he became the city's office assessor as well as path master.

When the War of 1812 broke out, rations were needed to feed troops stationed in New York and New Jersey. Elbert Anderson was a rations contractor for the war effort. He advertised for a subcontractor to provide 5,000 barrels of meat per year, and the Wilsons replied. It is at this point that the Uncle Sam story begins.

There are many different versions of how we got our Uncle. Every barrel of meat destined for the army had to be inspected and then labeled. Sam Wilson was the meat inspector for the northern army and marked the barrels E.A.-U.S. for Elbert Anderson and the United States. The meat was supplied mostly to troops stationed a little ways downriver, where soldiers knew of Sam Wilson and his nickname "Uncle Sam." They recognized the place of origin, and just assumed the initials were for Sam. Another version, recounted in the *New York Gazette* of May 12, 1830, states that it started when one of Sam's workmen, when asked what the E.A.-U.S. meant, just assumed it was for Elbert Anderson and Uncle Sam. Using the initials "U.S." was relatively new (like the country), and not familiar to most people. Another version, passed down by a great-nephew, said that visitors to Troy's docks would ask about the barrels and about Uncle Sam. An Irishman replied that Uncle Sam was "Uncle Sam Wilson. It is he who is feeding the army." (Alton Ketchum wrote *Uncle Sam: The Man and the Legend* in 1959. It was reprinted in 1975 for the bicentennial, and is usually available somewhere in the world of the interwebs. We found our copy on eBay. It is a very detailed biography of Sam's life and the history of "Uncle Sam.")

Samuel Wilson had a successful and fulfilling life in Troy. His health began to fail him in his 80s, and he died at 87 during a cholera epidemic in 1854. He was buried originally in Mount Ida Cemetery near his home, but later was interred at Oakwood Cemetery in Troy. There are no large statues on his grave, just a plaque commemorating his life. It is, however, festooned with dozens of American Flags. According to

Roadside America, some local Trojans believe that his real grave is next to the Route 2 Bridge in Troy near the housing project. When they checked this out, they apparently found a marble slab engraved with the dates of an earlier bridge. It looks like a gravestone, and it happens to have a New York State historical marker for Uncle Sam next to it, hence the confusion.

Samuel Wilson's house stood on Ferry Street on the western edge of Prospect Park until 1971, when the city tore it down. Oooops. Realizing that this probably was not the best decision, the city built nothing on the site, and an archeological dig was done in 1993, where they found a few pieces of the house and the intact chamber pot of Sam Wilson. This artifact is now on display at the Rensselaer County Historical Society, housed inside the Hart-Cluett House and Carr Building at 59 2nd Street, Troy. Best to call, 272-7232.

Drawings of "Uncle Sam" started appearing in the 1830s, but it wasn't until the Civil War and later that a recognizable character appeared. Thomas Nast, of Santa Claus and the GOP elephant fame, started drawing Uncle Sam with his top hat, coat jacket, and striped pants in the 1870s. The iconic "Uncle Sam, I Want You," from the recruitment posters of both world wars, was drawn by James Montgomery Flagg in 1917. According to the Library of Congress Works of Art Catalog of Copyright for 1917, the Uncle Sam Statue and Picture Co. of Troy owned the copyright to a statue called *Our Uncle Sam*, which was produced by the Boston Sculpture Company. We have not yet run into any of these in town. There is, however, a large aluminum sculpture of Uncle Sam, erected in 1980, at the entrance to Riverfront Park. There is a big plaque in front of this with the names of the 17 committee members who made the statue a reality, but no mention of the sculptor's name. If you look on the back of the sculpture, though, in very small capital letters, you will see the name K. George Kratina 1980. Kratina was a well-regarded sculptor and a beloved professor at RPI. He died the year the sculpture was completed.

Did You Know?

Long before there was an Uncle Sam, there was a Brother Jonathan. There's a well-passed-down story that the name came from Governor Jonathan Trumbull of Connecticut, a state that was a major source of supplies for the Revolutionary forces, and that when asked how we could win the war, George Washington supposedly said, "We must consult Brother Jonathan."

However, the name "Brother Jonathan" dates back to the 1600s and the early Puritan settlers. Although initially meant as an insult, it came to be a name for and embraced by all New Englanders, especially Yankee sailors (and peddlers). By 1842, with a weekly newspaper called *Brother Jonathan*, the character became well known in all of North America. He became an American symbol, as drawn by Thomas Nast, dressed in striped pants and a dark jacket and wearing a stovepipe hat. Nast did draw Uncle Sam as well, but look closely and you'll see that Brother Jonathan has a feather on his hat and is clean-shaven. Uncle Sam always had the goatee. When the Uncle Sam character was getting really popular after the 1870s, he stole Brother Jonathan's clothes, and Brother Jonathan disappeared. In New England, on occasion, you can still hear someone say, "We must consult Brother Jonathan."

History 101

The War of 1812

On June 18, 1812, President James Madison declared war on Great Britain. This was one way to remind them that hey, remember that other war? The one we fought for, and won, our independence in? Upset that Great Britain was restricting our trade with France just because they were at war with them, and snatching our seaman off American boats to sail for the Royal Navy, and then the whole attacking the USS *Chesapeake*, was just too much to sit back and take. Congress also thought it would be a cakewalk to cross the Canadian border and annex more territory. The Canadians thought otherwise and were aided by the British army and Native American tribes who were hoping to stop western expansion into their territories. General Henry Dearborn secured 300 acres, in what is now East Greenbush, to house 6,000 troops waiting to be sent north. This was the center of the northern offensive. The war raged on until the Treaty of Ghent was signed on February 17, 1815. The US lost more than 2,200 soldiers. Basically, the war ended in a draw, everything reverting back to the status quo. A few notable outcomes were the writing of "The Star Spangled Banner" (set to an English drinking song) at the Battle of Fort McHenry; the forging of a true national identity for Canadians; and the Native Americans being left without a European ally to fend off the settling of the West.

More Beer Here, and Bourbon, Rye, and Cider, Too

From the very beginning, beer has been part of the Capital District's lifeblood. Albany, being one of the colonies' oldest cities, had its breweries up and running before the city was even chartered. Good to have one's priorities right. With a clean river, hops growing wild in the woods, and land perfect for growing wheat, it was a brewer's dream. Anyone was able to brew any quantity they could for *personal consumption*. Breweries run as a business were subject to some regulations, and even with that, there were more than a dozen breweries operating in Beverwyck in the 1630s. Gansevoort, Van Curler, Vrooman, Schermerhorn—all were very early brewers whose names are still part of the local vocabulary. The Capital District saw a huge industrial boom in the 1850s, and with that a surge of immigrants. With this came a whole new selection of ales and lagers. Troy's Irish influx dominated the breweries there: Cleary, Kennedy, Dunn, Murphy, and Conway all had very successful operations. Scottish and English immigrants flooded the Albany brew scene. Although never getting as big as Troy and Albany, Schenectady did make moves into western New York thanks to the Erie Canal and was first in line when it came to getting imported ingredients flowing east. With the arrival of Edison's electric company, more beer was needed! For a short while, the beer business grew in Schenectady, the biggest brewer being the Mohawk Valley Brewing Company.

Things were great in the beer business until January 16, 1920. Prohibition ended it all for Schenectady. Troy became a distribution point for illegally imported alcohol from Canada, and in Albany, most breweries were forced to close or reinvent themselves as producers of near-beer or some other nonalcoholic beverage. Of course, rules were broken, and politicians and business leaders who took over some breweries continued producing full-strength beer, just sending it out from the basement doors, not out the front. The few Albany breweries that survived Prohibition—Hedrick's, Beverwyck/Schaefer, Dobler—were all gone by 1972. In Troy, the Quandt, Stanton Brothers, and Fitzgerald Brothers breweries were all gone by 1962. The Capital District without a beer of its own! Oh noooooo! And this is where we started over.

Bill Newman was responsible for the start of the craft-brewing industry in the Capital District in the early 1980s. He was actually the first on the East Coast. Interested in producing a different variety of beer and ale, he studied and perfected his craft and started producing his ale in small batches. He taught seminars to up-and-coming brewers like Jim Koch of Samuel Adams fame. Newman's brewery on Learned Street in Albany closed in the early '90s; he was just a little too early on the scene to make it big, but he provided the kick in the hindquarters that Albany needed to get things going. His Albany Amber and Winter Ale are fondly remembered.

Brewpubs started cropping up all over the Capital District, offering their own craft beers with food, and a couple of the originals are still here. Notable are **Brown's Brewing Co.** (originally Brown and Moran) and **C. H. Evans Brewing Co. at the Albany Pump Station**. Brown's was the first brewpub in the area, and after 20-plus years it is still one of the best places around to meet up with friends and have a great beer. Its historic building at 417 River Street in Troy has a beautiful view of the Hudson, great food, live music, and, oh yeah, more than 25 unique ales and lagers brewed on-site (at least 10 of which are available on draught any given day). Their award list is so long you can look it up yourself. Housed in another cool historic building, this one in Albany, **The Albany Pump Station** at 19 Quackenbush Square is another friendly place to meet and catch up. Great menu, great prices, great beer. Neil Evans revived the family business, C. H. Evans Brewing Company of Hudson, which produced beer from 1786 until Prohibition closed them down in 1920.

Today, the brewery makes at least a dozen kinds of beer on premises, including the award winning Kick-Ass Brown Ale. Newer craft breweries include Mad Jack Brewing Co. at **The Van Dyck Lounge**, 237 Union Street, Schenectady. The Van Dyck maintains its lovely, jazzy atmosphere, but now serves up an assortment of unique craft beers. And adding to the appeal of Albany's Warehouse District, **Druthers** (whose flagship brewpub opened in Saratoga Springs in 2012) has a second location at 1053 Broadway in Albany, giving us another reason to stay downtown and share a choice, award-winning beer and good meal.

Another outstanding addition to the craft distilling business is the **Albany Distilling Co.,** located next to the Albany Pump Station at 78 Montgomery Street. From their beginnings as two guys with a still, John Curtin and Matthew Jager (now a partner at **Yankee Distillers in Clifton Park**—excellent rye whiskey here by the way), have produced a line of distinctive, New York-grain-based craft spirits. Their aged whiskeys are a real treat. Everything is made in Albany, and you are welcome to schedule a tour or to come to a tasting. The address looks like a warehouse, because it is, but just go through the door—it has a sign on it—and up the ramp to the distillery. They are looking into larger digs so check online first to see if they are home. **Nine Pin Ciderworks** at 929 Broadway, also in Albany's Warehouse District, is another example of the entrepreneurial spirit that is alive and well in Albany. You can find their delicious signature hard ciders all over town, but at their tasting room on Broadway, you can enjoy a sampling of an ever-changing array of in-house experimental hard ciders. Dozens of them. Tours by appointment, 449-9999; tasting hours are Wednesday through Friday from 4 to 9 p.m., and Saturday 1 to 9 p.m.

Lucky for you, if you hit upon a favorite at the brewery, there's a good chance you can find it on tap at one of the dozens of craft beer houses around the area. Depending on your age and sensibilities, you will find a place that fits. From our friends and family, we suggest **City Beer Hall**, 42 Howard Street, Albany—it's in the name, plus it has really good food; **The Merry Monk**, 90 Pearl Street, Albany, good everything *and* mussels; **The Lionheart Pub**, 448 Madison Avenue, Albany, an Albany staple with a great beer selection; **The Ruck** at 104 Third Street in Troy—always a new beer and great food; **Footsy Magoos** at 17 First Street in Troy, great feel and food; **Centre Street Pub**, 613 Union Street, Schenectady—big, everything you want, and music on Friday and Saturday; **Pinhead Susan's**, 38–40 Broadway, Schenectady—a great Irish bar, featuring Mad Jack brews from the Van Dyke, good food, and music. We have to mention **Wolff's Biergarten**, 895 Broadway in Albany, 165 Erie Boulevard in Schenectady, and 2 King Street in Troy, because there's beer there, lots of it. It's mostly German and Belgian, but it's good, and the place is really fun.

Just so we don't hurt anyone's feelings, we have to say that there are more than a couple of dozen craft beer breweries "around" the Capital Region just not "in" the Capital District. The Beer Diviner, Wolf Hollow Brewing, Olde Saratoga, Chatham Brewing, and Shmaltz Brewing Co. are just a few whose excellent craft beers are available in local bars and markets.

Art in Plein Site

Don't feel like spending the day in an art gallery but still want to enjoy some art? It's pretty easy to stumble over a few things just by walking around town. Albany sort of wins the prize in this category, mostly because of the modern art collection at the Empire State Plaza.

Governor Nelson Rockefeller's mother was one of the founders of the Museum of Modern Art in New York City in 1929, and he became president of the museum's board of trustees in 1939, so he had a real in on who the up-and-comers were. The Empire State Plaza collection consists of 92 paintings and sculptures, which adorn the concourse and the plaza itself. It includes Jackson Pollock's *Number 12, 1952* and an untitled Mark Rothko. There are two Alexander Calder sculptures, one in the Corning Tower lobby, and one, *Triangles and Arches*, perched over the reflecting pool. You can get the full list of pieces on the Office of General Services website. We own them, so we all should enjoy them. Also in the plaza is the haunting New York State Fallen Firefighters Memorial by Robert Eccleston.

Hop over to Lafayette Park, where the lovingly restored Albany County Vietnam Veterans Monument by Merlin Szosz graces Capitol Hill. Nearby in Academy Park, you will find the statue of local scientist extraordinaire Joseph Henry. John Flanagan, who designed the Washington quarter in 1932, designed this statue in 1927. Across from the statue, closer to the court building, is a large fountain installed in 1988 by the Albany Beautification Committee (we had one of these!).

Across from Academy Park at City Hall is the statue of Philip Schuyler, given to the city by George C. Hawley in memory of his wife Theodora in 1925. Inside the base, there is a chest with mementos, including a picture of Mrs. Hawley. The sculptor, J. Massey Rhind, was also the sculptor of Washington Park's most famous landmark, the Moses fountain. In 1878, Henry L. King left a sum of $20,000 to build a memorial to his father, Rufus Henry King, based on the bible story of Moses at the Rock of Horab. Rufus Henry King was a wealthy merchant and later, president of the Albany Savings Bank. It was unveiled in 1893 and has been a city favorite since.

The Robert Burns statue, or the McPherson Legacy to the City of Albany, was unveiled in Washington Park on September 30, 1888, to celebrate the great Scottish poet. Mary McPherson was the last surviving member of her family in Albany, and had inherited all of the money her father earned as janitor of the State House as well as her brother's savings from the same job. This combined with her own money earned from working as a housemaid totaled about $40,000. At the urging of her friends in Albany's Scottish community, she decided to leave the bulk of her estate in the hands of her trusted executors to erect a statue that would be "a monument worthy of the man, an ornament to the park, and an honor to the land of my birth." The sculptor was Charles Calverley of New York (born in Albany), and the price was $24,000. Mary McPherson died before it was built.

Down on Broadway between Clinton and State there is a wealth of public art, from the statue of Mayor Thomas Whalen with his dog Finn McCool and a tricentennial version of our city seal (both by Hy Rosen of *Times Union* cartoon fame) in Tricentennial Park, to the clock over Union Station, which took years to complete. The old post office on the east side of Broadway (now the James T. Foley United States Courthouse) has an amazing frieze designed by Albert T. Stewart, which depicts postal services, customs duties, and court missions. The post office moved out in 1995, and now US District Court, US Marshals, Customs, and the FBI share the building. *Do not take pictures of this building.* It makes them very grumpy.

Don't overlook the architecture here. The SUNY Plaza building is covered in amazing little sculptures and gargoyles, as well as a fabulous weathervane, so make sure you look up. The electroliers in front of the State Education Department building by Charles Keck are terrific. There is way too much to list, so we strongly suggest you get your hands on a copy of *Albany Architecture: A Guide to the City*, by Waite, Gold, and McCarty, from 1993. It has a wealth of information as well as a zillion photos.

The Hudson River Way is an outdoor gallery all on its own. Every one of the 30 lampposts has an original trompe l'oeil still life recalling Albany's history.

Over in Troy, the architecture is the real star, so walk around and keep your eyes open. They are really getting a lot of the best old buildings in shape these days, including the old Proctor's Theater at 90 4th St. (Troy had a Proctor's too, just like Schenectady). The gargoyles are fantastic on this one. Just look up past the lions. The Cinema Art Theatre on River Street ended its career as an X-rated movie house, and was shut down in 2006; it is still a very cool looking building. A spooky-looking place is the old Gasholder Building, in Troy's Little Italy at the corner of 5th Avenue and Jefferson Street. The trees have gotten tall, so in the summer you might not even notice this giant, circular building, plunked down at the end of a residential street.

Troy is famous for the number of Tiffany windows it has. St. Paul's Episcopal Church has spectacular Tiffany windows and chandeliers. You can stop in to see them during Troy Night Out (the last Friday of every month) or during Sunday services. The Troy Public Library also boasts a Tiffany over the circulation desk.

In the center of town, you will find the Soldiers and Sailors Monument in Monument Square. This is a 50-foot-tall column topped with a 17-foot statue of the goddess Columbia, modeled by James E. Kelly. The monument was designed by the Fuller and Wheeler firm of Albany, and finished at the end of the 19th century. It was rededicated in 1991. There are bronze relief panels all around the base depicting battle scenes. It is usually decked out in lights during the holiday season.

The aluminum statue of a stylized Uncle Sam greets you as you head into Riverfront Park off River Street. This was completed in 1980, the same year the sculptor, K. George Kratina, died. Kratina was a professor at RPI and had his studio in Old Chatham. A 1922 press release called him a boy genius.

There are a few wall murals around Troy that add to the old-time feel here. Brown's Brewing Company has a beauty on the side of its building, there's one on the side of Pfiel Hardware, and there is another very large mural across from the Troy Music Hall. Walk through the RPI campus to the Greene building and enjoy the magical kinetic sculpture by George Rickey gracing the lawn.

On to Schenectady, where the buildings are also the things to notice. Proctors is wonderful inside and out, thanks to the preservation efforts of the Arts Center & Theatre of Schenectady (ACT). Gorgeous gilt work and murals make it easy to wait for the show to start. City Hall, at 105 Jay Street, is another great building. Built during the Depression (1931–33), it was not cheap and was referred to as "Fagal's Folly" after the mayor, Henry Fagal. It's a really classic-looking building, designed by the firm of McKim, Mead & White from New York City. It's got a square clock tower on top with a gold cupola on top of that. We really like the back of this building the best, so walk all the way around. In 1978 this building was added to the National Register of Historic Places. On the Union campus, the Nott Memorial, built in 1858 in memory of the college's president, Eliphalet Nott, became a National Historic Landmark in 1986. It is fabulous.

One of the great things about Schenectady is the number of old "ghost signs" of businesses and products painted on the sides of buildings. Our favorite is the Coca-Cola sign on a building on Broadway. Someone is keeping this one up, and we love it.

In the little Liberty Park at the corner of State Street and Washington Avenue, you will find one of the 200 100-inch copper replicas of the Statue of Liberty that were given to communities across America by the Boy Scouts during the early 1950s. Also, welcoming you to Schenectady is a terrific black metal sign with a very descriptive design of the Schenectady massacre and fire of 1690.

One of our favorite statues in the historic Stockade District is that of Lawrence the Indian. Lawrence was supposed to have aided the surviving settlers after the massacre in 1690 by going after the French to rescue prisoners and negotiating with Canada for their release. He urged the settlers to come back and rebuild. The statue was ordered from the catalog of the J.L. Mott Iron Works, and was known as No. 53 Indian Chief (25 others of this model have been found worldwide). It was erected at the intersections of Front, Ferry, and Green Streets in the Stockade on September 12, 1887. He wasn't called Lawrence until 1962; he was known simply as "the Indian," a place to meet or use in directions (go east from the Indian). It was then he became "Lawrence the Maquaise," the Stockade's guardian. He was taken down and cleaned fairly recently, but now he's back up in the middle of the Stockade District where he belongs.

Don't forget to visit Albany Rural, Oakwood, and Vale Cemeteries for their remarkable stonework.

Mind, Body, Planet

Mind

The best way to keep your brain up and running is to use it. Learn something new. Two of our favorite things are music and food. Lucky for you, you can get better at both with all of the classes offered in and around the tri-cities.

Cooking

We love food, and any way to make it better, healthier, and faster is all good to us. There are a lot of places to learn some new techniques right in town, so here goes.

The Arts Center of the Capital Region: 265 River Street, Troy, 273-0552. They have a culinary arts program that gets you cooking with local chefs and bakers, with some afternoon and some evening classes. Check their website for course offerings. They all sound good. http://www.artscenteronline.org/culinary-arts/

Gio Culinary Studio: 22 South Main Street, Voorheesville, 391-2323. From pastry to cheese, you can select a class that will teach you just the specialty you want. Some afternoon classes, but mostly in the evenings. Just Google Gio Culinary Studio to see what classes are available, or go to http://www.gioculinarystudio.com/oscommerce1/catalog/.

The Cooking School @ Market Bistro: 873 New Loudon Road, Latham, 782-0441. Yes this is Price Chopper's cooking school, but have you ever eaten at Market Bistro? The food is amazing. They have a kitchen classroom right there with an ever-changing list of classes.

Check to see what's coming up at https://www.marketbistro.com/CookingSchool/Home/About.

Albany Cooking School: Different Drummer's Kitchen Co., Stuyvesant Plaza, Albany, 459-7990. Some are instructional classes and some are more hands-on. Check to see who the instructor is and ask how the class is run. Full range of classes. You can have your birthday party here too. http://www.differentdrummerskitchen.com/store/pc/viewcontent.asp?idpage=1

Spoon & Wisk: Watkins Plaza, 1675 Route 9, Clifton Park, 371-4450. This is another nice kitchen supply store with some really appealing evening classes. They fill up fast, so sign up early at http://spoonandwisk.com/main/index.php?m=1&p=6.

Special Note: Look for another cooking school opening in 2016–17 in Troy. **Culinary Square** at 251 River Street, 326-5818, is hoping to get classes up and running sometime in the next year. In the meantime, you can shop for great kitchen supplies and accessories from this mother-daughter owned shop.

If you are getting really serious about this cooking stuff, **Schenectady County Community College** offers a top-notch two-year culinary arts program. The school is located at 78 Washington Avenue in downtown Schenectady, 381-1200. Hungry? You can try out the students' cooking at the Casola Dining Room on the first floor of Elston Hall on campus.

Music

Learning to play an instrument is another way to keep the gray cells up to speed. There are a lot of places that have been around a long time, and some new ones that can help you do just that.

Piper's Dojo: 11 North Pearl Street, Albany, 855-529-3656. If you've ever wanted to master the bagpipes—and really, who hasn't?—this is a great place to do that. **Dojo University** is an online classroom for all levels of players with clear, instructive videos that you can play over and over until you get it. Unlike most bagpipe do-it-yourself methods, where you do nothing but boring exercises, they have music you can play right off the bat. The best part of this program, for us, is that you can practice in your own place when no one is home, and only the dog will give you grief. You can order any piping supplies from the online store. If you want a real live lesson, they have a list of trusted instructors. For any repairs, they will refer you to a local pipemaker. http://pipersdojo.com or www.dojouniversity.com.

Carondelet Music Center: 385 Watervliet-Shaker Road, Latham, 783-3608. Sponsored by the Sisters of St. Joseph of Carondelet, this music school has been around for more than 20 years. Classes in most instruments and voice are taught by the sisters, as well as lay people with a degree or music-teaching background. Lessons are paid for over a 14-week semester system in spring and fall. You can join a group lesson or have a private one. CMC is known for its Kindermusik program, which has been given a "Maestro" rating, meaning it's in the top 5 percent of Kindermusik programs worldwide. These are music and movement classes for babies right up to seven-year-olds. Same semester plan, but there are hour-long summer camp classes as well. Check them out at http://www.carondeletmusiccenter.com/.

Parkway Music: 1777 Route 9, Clifton Park, 383-0300. Music lessons are available everyday from an outstanding group of musicians. The best drummer we know took his lessons here and loved them. The selection of new and used instruments and equipment is fantastic. We got a pair of amps here years ago and they are still onstage today, complete with the original owner's band name stenciled across the front. "Whalin Bones," are you still out there? parkwaymusic.com

The Music Studio: 1237 Central Avenue, Albany, 459-7799. Piano is the focus of this school, offering group lessons to children as young as four, and private lessons through high school age. During the school's 35-year run in the Capital District, it has developed its own curriculum that teaches music fundamentals as well as expertise on the instrument. You start with their "Foundation" program, and once completed, you can move up to their "Piano Program." For adults, they offer a "Recreational Piano" program to catch up on what you have forgotten or to start from scratch in a group format. http://themusicstudio.com

Troy Music Academy: 9 3rd Street, Troy, 285-0145. Lessons on a full range of instruments, tailored to the individual student. They also have a Kindermusik program. You can book one lesson at a time or get a discount if you sign up for recurring weekly lessons. http://troy musicacademy.com

Drome Sound: 1875 State Street, Schenectady, 370-3701. Drome has been around for decades. Professional musicians offer lessons on a wide variety of instruments in every style from classical to heavy metal. You can also find the guitar of your dreams hanging in one of their racks. We've gotten some very cool guitars here. http://dromesound.com

Hilton Music Center: 104 Colonie Center, 459-9400. We took our drum lessons here when they were LA Hilton Music in the Latham Circle Mall. Same people, good staff, fun lessons, and a whole store of instruments for you to shop for. hiltonmusiccenter.com

Magic of Music: 341 Delaware Avenue, Delmar, 475-0215. This music school has been in the Albany area for more than 30 years. They have a good reputation for quality lessons on any number of instruments and voice. They can also help with the preparation of your NYSSMA solos. Parents, you know what that is. http://magicofmusicstudio.com

There are a lot of private instructors around. We suggest that if you have any theater or musician friends, ask them if they have someone they love, and go from there.

Miscellany

Learning to sew at **Jo-Ann Fabric and Craft Store**, or to dance at **eba** on Hudson at Lark in Albany or at one of the continuing-education classes offered by local school districts, are fun. Bring friends and it's even better. Same goes for **Paint & Sip**, in Latham and Saratoga, where you can create your own masterpiece while enjoying your favorite wine or beer. **Hudson Valley Community College** has an ever-changing selection of classes in its continuing-ed program, from writing workshops to kickboxing. They also have a summer circus school. Check them out at communityed@hvcc.edu.

If you prefer a quieter way to enhance your mind, try meditation. The **Shambala Meditation Center of Albany** will teach you what it is and how to do it (747 Madison Avenue, Albany, 729-4055).

Body

We all have one, and most of us don't take very good care of it. You have to start by eating well. The Capital District is lucky to have some outstanding farmer's markets, many year-round, that offer you fresh, natural, *local* food. Start eating well and you'll become an all-new you. Our favorites are:

Troy Waterfront Farmer's Market: River Street in the summer, Uncle Sam Atrium in the winter. Saturdays, 9–2. This is one of our favorite markets any time of year. Over 80 vendors with all kinds of fresh everything. There are a number of CSA (community supported agriculture) farms—Our Farm, Denison, and Homestead Farms—where you can buy a share of their produce at the beginning of the season and pick up fresh produce from them all season. Buy fresh milk from Battenkill Valley Creamery; fresh meats direct from the farm; wine from our local vineyards; fish, flowers, jams, honey, bread from Troy's own Placid Baker; prepared foods, and so much more. The best part of this market is that everyone seems so happy to be there! It is a good time from start to finish.

Schenectady Greenmarket: Jay Street around City Hall in the summer, Proctors in the winter. Sundays, 10–2. This is another market we love. Large selection of everything here too: produce, Nine Pin hard cider, cheeses, peanut butter, fresh pesto, meat, breads, dairy, and a great place to sit and enjoy the music. The eclectic selection of little shops along Jay Street just adds to the appeal.

The Crossings: 580 Albany Shaker Road, Colonie. Saturdays, 9–1, May–September. As this one has grown, a lot of the great area vendors have been joining in. Fresh produce, perennials, cheese, Nine Pin cider, etc. They've added more parking, so it's not as hard to find a spot. One of the big pluses for this market is the park it's in. There are miles of paved paths for walking and biking, and you can cross-country ski in the winter. There is a wonderful playground, a garden maze, and a pond to enjoy. Your pup is also welcome as long as you pick up after him.

Empire State Plaza Farmer's Market: At the plaza, Madison Avenue at Eagle Street. Outdoors, May-October; indoors in the concourse, November–April. The summer market runs 10–2 on Wednesdays and Fridays; the winter market is Wednesdays only, 11–2. If you are stuck downtown, this market has a lot to offer with fresh, local produce and meats you can pick up during your lunch break. It also turns the plaza into something green and wonderful a couple of days a week.

There are a lot more markets all over the area, and even ones selling right out of their community garden plots. You will be able to find one close to home. Check the weekly *Preview* section of the *Times Union* or just look for signs along the road that pop up in late spring.

Exercise Time!

You can get a good workout at any number of gyms in the area. The **Rudy A. Ciccotti Family Recreation Center** in Colonie has a full range of family-friendly facilities and classes, including spin classes, swimming, basketball, and yoga; **The Revolution,** now in Loudonville as well as Clifton Park, can give you a great cardio workout; **The Hot Yoga Spot** is now open in Latham, Albany, East Greenbush, Saratoga, and Clifton Park when you want a little heat with your yoga. And there are plenty of other gyms, like **Vent Fitness**, as well as your local **YMCA** or **JCC**, but have you ever considered something a little more challenging, even a little risky? Here is a list of a few exercise options you may have never considered:

Spelunking: You know, crawling into a dark cave to explore with just the lamp on your helmet (and a spare). There are actually nearby caves in the Capital District where you can do this. In most cases, this should be done in groups, so you'll want to join a "grotto." **The Helderberg-Hudson Grotto** (hhg@caves.org) meets every month to plan trips, train, and work on cave rescue, mapping, etc. There really is a National Speleological Society, which can hook you up with a grotto in your area. The **Northeastern Cave Conservancy** currently maintains 15 caves after acquiring "Benson's Cave" in 2014. Their website will tell you about each of the caves (http://www.necaveconservancy.org).

Fencing: OK, so you picture yourself more as a swashbuckler than a bat. You can learn to master the épée or sabre at a number of places. One is **Capital District Fencing School**, at 1840 Van Vranken Avenue, Schenectady; call James for épée (248-5002), Mark for sabre (879-2716). Classes for all ages and skill levels. **Beaches Sabre Club:** 73 4th Street, Troy, 273-7466. Beaches will get you up to competitive levels, but if you want to learn just for the fun of it, you are equally welcome (http://www. beachesny.net). At **RPI Fencing Club**, classes are open to the public, and the fees are low. They meet twice a week during the school year and supply everything you need except your glove. Practice classes are in the RPI Armory on 15th Street in Troy. Questions? fencing@union. rpi.edu

Triathlon Clubs: So you think you're ready to become an ironman/woman? You are going to need some good training and support if you plan on spending a day swimming 0.47 miles, racing a bicycle for 12 miles, and finishing up with a quick 3.1-mile run. And that's the easy race. The full-on ironman race will have you swimming 2.4 miles, racing 112 miles on your bicycle, followed by a nice 26.2 mile run—all in one day. The **Capital District Triathlon Club** holds training sessions in and around Crystal Lake at Crystal Cove, Averill Park. Open to members and nonmembers, the 12-week summer session helps you get in shape and to ready yourself for upcoming races. The club meets year round and uses the off-season for members to catch up with each other and plan for next year (http://www.cdtriclub.org). The **Bethlehem Tri Club** (BTC), which promotes the sport for all levels of competition, also has a summer training series, usually at Warners Lake in the Helderbergs. They also meet year round and join for indoor spinning classes to keep in shape (http://www.bethlehemtriclub.com). Serious/interested runners and bicyclists can join the **Albany Running Exchange**, a 1,200-member running club that offers daily group runs, races, and camaraderie for all ages (www.albanyrunningexchange.org), or the **Mohawk Hudson Cycling Club**, a 700-member club that sponsors road bike rides around the region (www.mohawkhudsoncyclingclub.org). Pick up a free copy of *Adirondack Sports and Fitness* at the Albany Visitors Center for a list of area clubs and competitions.

Trampolining: You know that when you have to sign a waiver before you get inside it's going to be way fun. We have two indoor trampoline parks in the Albany area. Both offer wall-to-wall trampoline jumping fields, foam pits, and other ways for you to get flying. Usually, it's less than the cost of a movie to get an hour of bounce time. **Sky Zone Trampoline Park** is at 50 Simmons Lane, Albany, 417-3838, www.skyzone.com/

albany; and **Flight Trampoline Park** is at 30A Post Road, Colonie, 952-0433, www.albanyflighttrampolinepark.com/.

Horseback Riding: Recreational trail rides are not available in the Capital District unless you own your own horse on your own farm or board it at somebody else's. You need to travel up to Lake Luzerne or Lake Placid for recreational riding. But, if you are interested in learning horsemanship for pleasure or competition, there are places nearby that can teach you. Most have boarding facilities as well. **Winter Glen**, run forever by Peggy Aedjian, sits on 40 acres with both an indoor and outdoor arena. Lessons for all levels of riders (and horses). Winter Glen is at 7296 Guilderland Avenue, Guilderland, 356-3364, http://www.winterglenfarm.com. Another one that's been around awhile is **Dutch Manor**, at 2331 Western Avenue, Guilderland, 456-5010. It's more of a show barn, with lessons and boarding. **4M's Farm** is at 2537 Phillips Road, Castleton, 477-5470, http://www.4msfarm.net/. This place has a really relaxed feel to it. Lessons are fun; horses are great. This is a Western, rather than an English barn, with an outdoor arena and trails. Nice place to start if you've never ridden before. **Placid Hills Farm** is a beautiful, relatively new horsemanship facility located at 196 Town Office Road in Brunswick, 279-9717, http://www.placidhillsstables.com. Private lessons, multiple arenas, acres of turnout, trails, even Wi-Fi in their lounge. There are more out there; ask your friends or Google "horseback riding in the Albany area."

Planet

If you feel the need to commune with the local flora and fauna, you will find a number of

Note: Be advised: fauna also includes biting flies, which are abundant in the summer months.

nature conservancies, arboretums, parks, and even cemeteries where you can commune all you want.

Pine Hollow Arboretum: 16 Maple Avenue, Slingerlands, 439-6472. This is a 25-acre gem a few miles outside of Albany. Don't be confused when you pull up to the address. It looks like someone's home—because it is. Dr. Abbuhl has carefully planted (and labeled) thousands of trees intermixed with beautiful ponds and running water. It is now a member-supported not-for-profit arboretum. There are trails throughout, places to sit and meditate, and a visitor's center for information. The trails are open every day from dawn to dusk, and the visitor's center is open Saturday and Sunday, April through October. Individual membership is $25 a year. A $5 donation is suggested for nonmembers.

Hollyhock Hollow Sanctuary: 46 Rarick Road, Selkirk. This is one of those amazing places you've never heard of, that you will fall in love with. This 140-acre estate was bequeathed to Audubon International by Leona and Robert Rienow, Ph.D. (a SUNY Albany professor). Although Audubon moved to the Rensselaer Tech Park in 2013, the trails are still maintained and filled with birds you are not likely to see anywhere else. The walk along the Onesquethaw Creek is a favorite. Some of Dr. Rienow's original hand-painted signs still mark special places along the paths. Open year round from dawn to dusk. Free.

Christman Sanctuary: 3281 Schoharie Turnpike, Duanesburg. Will and Catherine Christman started to preserve their farm as a nature sanctuary in 1888. The original 97 acres was bought by the Nature Conservancy in 1970, and has since been added to. If hiking along the lovely Bozenkill Creek, punctuated by assorted waterfalls, sounds idyllic to you, then here's your place. The trails are not long and not too hard, and bring you over streams, through rocks, and up and down on stone or wooden steps. Christman set out to create a plantation of different varieties of trees, including locust, cedar, spruce, and red and white pine. There are traces of his old orchards along the trails, too; you'll notice these when you see the apples on the ground. Like other nature preserves in the area, this one is maintained by volunteers, including the Mohawk Valley Hiking Club. Open year round, dawn to dusk. The waterfalls are more spectacular in the spring but beautifully frozen over in the winter. The parking area holds only a few cars, so if you can get here on a weekday, you'll have a better shot at a parking place. Free.

Lisha Kill Natural Area: 2518 Rosendale Road, Niskayuna. This is another preserve obtained by the Nature Conservancy between 1964 and 1966, saving it from highway expansion. Its 108 acres, virtually right off Route 7, contain a 40-acre old-growth forest, running streams, and deep ravines. It has a couple of miles of trails, not too hard but with lots of roots sticking up, within what seems a deep and dark forest—beautiful. Most preserves do not allow pets, but you can bring your leashed dog to this one. It is open year round from dawn to dusk, but may have days when it closes due to dangerous trail conditions. Free.

Five Rivers Environmental Education Center: 56 Game Farm Road, Delmar, 475-0291. This is one of the more family-friendly places to go and hike. There's an information center with, most important, bathrooms and decent parking. This 446-acre preserve is run by the New York State Department of Environmental Conservation and pretty much has it all. There are over 12 miles of easy hiking trails through all kinds of habitats, 16 ponds, fields, orchards, and woods supporting hundreds of species of birds, mammals, and creepy-crawly things.

Albany Pine Bush Discovery Center: 195 New Karner Road, Albany, 456-0655. This is the gateway to a pine barren encompassing 3,000 acres of well-marked trails through one of the last remaining historical landscapes of the Capital District. Schenectady means "place beyond the pines," and it has been that for centuries. This is a special ecosystem, which is home to the endangered Karner Blue butterfly. The Discovery Center will introduce you to the preserve, and then you can discover it for yourself. Although the preserve is big, the noise from the surrounding highways and nearby shooting range distract from what could be a perfect escape from the real world.

John Boyd Thacher State Park and the Emma Treadwell Thacher Nature Center: 1 Hailes Cave Road, or off Route 157 in Voorheesville, 872-1237. Over 2,000 acres in the hills overlooking Albany. The Indian Ladder Trail takes you along the Helderberg Escarpment and is not to be missed. It is open for hiking from spring through fall, but there are also about 25 miles of trails throughout the park that remain open year round. You can hike, mountain bike, cross-country ski, snowshoe, or snowmobile here. Thompson's Lake Campground has 140 campsites if you want to stay over. Watch out for bats—they make their home in the caves here. The Nature Center is also open year round (closed

Mondays and holidays), which is great if you are with kids, as they have a lot of hands-on stuff.

The Albany Rural Cemetery: 48 Cemetery Avenue, Menands; **Oakwood Cemetery**: 186 Oakwood Avenue, Troy; and **Vale Cemetery and Park**: 907 State Street, Schenectady. All of these are old cemeteries laid out as magnificent parks. Because they are all in town, you don't need to travel to get back to nature. Oakwood is 400 acres of splendor—beautiful landscaping, ponds, chapels, and history galore. Albany Rural is home to many of the city's who's who, or who were. Walking its 467 acres surrounded by amazing monuments takes you right back in time. At 100 acres, Vale is the smallest, but it has the same elements that make a walk a nature experience. Vale has Potter's Field as well as a special Union College plot for no-longer-with-us full professors and their families. Vandalism has really damaged a lot of the wonderful old monuments here, but the "black angel" is still intact and still watches over the Veeder family.

Google can give you all the information you need on a number of other great places in the Capital District. You just need to know what to Google. Here's a list of other places we enjoy: **Dyken Pond, Grafton Lakes, Normanskill Farm, Washington Park, Schuyler Flats Cultural Park, Lions Park** (in Niskayuna), **The Crossings, Corning Preserve, and the George Landis Arboretum.**

Did You Know?

The Nature Conservancy was incorporated in 1951. It was formerly called the Ecologists Union, and its mission was to take action to preserve threatened natural areas. The Nature Conservancy of Eastern New York was the first chapter to receive a charter, in 1954. It is one of the most trusted of the nonprofits in the world.

More Things You Can Do to Go Greener

We doubt Congress could agree on how to tie a shoelace, let alone save the planet, so it's up to us to do what we can to make sure we'll continue to have a place to live.

1. Lightbulbs, lightbulbs, lightbulbs. Last time we told you to switch to compact fluorescents, but now that LEDs have come down in price and could outlive you, it makes no sense to stick with the old incandescent bulbs. LEDs now have a full range of wattages and colors. Switch today.

2. When we walked around the house to see what kind of "vampire" electric use was going on, we were amazed at how many things are on standby waiting for us to use them. Besides the TV, computer, printer, and stereo,

some toasters watch and wait for you, too. We know it's great to not have to wait a whole minute for something to warm up, but you really are just making the electric company richer. Get in the habit of turning things off for the night and make the first one up in the morning go around and turn them back on.

3. Oven tips. Don't preheat unless you are making something sensitive like popovers and it matters (see recipe for popovers on page 121). Pizza and frozen entrees can just go in and take a few minutes longer. Don't open the door to check on the food; you lose 25 degrees with each peek.

4. Skip meat once a week. It takes 2,500 gallons of water to produce one pound of beef. Besides, a good mac and cheese is a great alternative.

5. Buy some nice cotton napkins and *use* them. We each go through about 2,000 napkins per year, which all end up in a landfill.

6. National Grid likes to send us letters telling us how terribly we are doing compared to our neighbors as far as heating goes. We happen to have the only old house in the neighborhood, with old windows and old doors, and many ways for winter to join us inside. But we really hated being the worst, so we did some cheap and easy fixes that got us a "great job" letter this winter. First, we got some of that plastic sheeting and tape to cover our windows. It's easy to install, easy to remove, and not that horribly visible. It really took care of the drafts. We installed those brush sweepers for the bottom of the doors and

put some thin foam insulation around them. The best fix
was our version of the European Radiator Booster, which
essentially pulls the heat from behind old radiators and
directs it into the room. We just put a window fan on
a stepstool in front of the radiator, and blew the warm
air into the room and toward our thermostat. The whole
house felt better and our gas usage went way down.

7. Curtains can also help keep the heat inside and the cold
out. If you needed an excuse to redecorate, this one will
probably pay for itself.

8. If you can plant things, plant them. Lots of them. Trees
clean the air and make oxygen. If you plant fruit or nut
trees, they can feed you, too. Start your own veggies from
seeds. We recommend Baker Creek Heirloom Seed Co.
for a full selection of untreated seeds for vegetables and
flowers. Not harmful for the bees or you. We started
everything from seeds, including onions, strawberries, and
a number of heirloom tomatoes, all with great success. It
will give you a way to get your hands dirty in February
while you wait for spring.

9. Coffee and tea grinds make great fertilizer. Save them up
and mix them in with your garden.

10. Please stop using pesticides on your lawns. Dandelions
herald the coming of spring, last just a little while,
and then are gone. Your pesticides kill your neighbor's
perennials, flow into our common water supply, and
sooner or later, will be proven to be carcinogenic or
worse.

11. Get your car a tune-up and make sure your tires are inflated correctly. Check seasonally. Tire pressure really does affect mileage.

12. Think before you shop or eat out. Bring your own bags for supplies and your own containers to bring home the leftovers. By using your own reusable containers you won't be adding to the piles of Styrofoam in the landfill.

13. If you have pets, you have to deal with the cat litter problem. We had been using a clay-based clumping litter, but the dust and stickiness of it really bothered us. Guest dogs tended to dine out of the litter box, and rather than face an intestinal emergency, we started using chicken feed instead. Layer feed or crumbles come in 50-pound bags at farm supply stores, clump pretty well, have very little dust, smell much better, and can actually be put out on the compost pile. They are also way cheaper.

14. Holiday suggestions. If you think using an artificial tree is better for the environment, it really isn't. Tree farms grow them to be cut. They plant more. Your pink aluminum tree will end up in a landfill and stay there forever. Reuse wrapping paper; recycle cards into gift cards for next year. When you gather around the old hearth, remember,

artificial fire logs emit 75 percent less carbon monoxide and 80 percent fewer dust particles than a real log. They are also about twice as efficient as real wood.

15. Use bars of soap instead of plastic dispensers. The paper wrap is recyclable, and you know the plastic really isn't.

16. Two-stroke power leaf blowers are the devil's plaything. They emit as much smog as 17 cars per hour. Put them away where no one has to listen to them whine and get some good cardio raking up your leaves by hand. Don't want to rake? Fine. Use your lawnmower to mulch up the leaves while you mow the lawn for the last time of the season.

17. Avoid air fresheners made with chemicals, and look for natural replacements in beeswax candles or dried lavender or eucalyptus leaves. Get some houseplants to suck up some of the harmful things in the air.

18. Switch to cellulose sponges. They are all-natural, bio-degradable, and not soaked in assorted chemicals that end up in rivers and streams.

19. Go solar if you can. There are still rebates. Solarize Troy is trying to make it easier for you. Now that Tesla is making a home storage battery, you could actually store your own power and be king of your own castle.

20. Before you bid your last farewell and your family turns you into a toxic dump site, think about a greener way to make your exit. Check with the Green Burial Council for some ideas. Schenectady's Vale Cemetery is a member.

Remember to recycle whenever you can. Share what you don't need. Use less. Plan for a sustainable future.

How to Make a Great Popover

The only trick for great popovers is to warm your eggs and milk to room temperature before you mix. You can microwave the milk to speed this up, but not too much.

You will need a deep (not wide) muffin pan. Spray with Pam or coat with Crisco. Preheat oven to 450 degrees.

For 6 big popovers:
1 cup flour
1 cup milk
¼ teaspoon salt
2 extra large or jumbo eggs

Mix eggs and milk together. Whisk in the flour and salt. We do this by hand and not with a mixer. Pour equal parts in the muffin tin. Bake for 15 minutes at 450 degrees and then turn down the heat to 350 and bake another 20 minutes. Double the recipe for 12.

Some of our friends like to get creative with these and add things before they are baked, like cheese. The basic recipe is perfect, but experiment if you like. Just start at room temperature.

Science 101

The snapping turtle is New York State's official reptile. The legislature voted overwhelmingly to approve this in 2006 based on a vote from elementary school kids. The snapping turtle is aggressive, will hiss at you before it bites you, and has claws that can inflict painful lacerations. Instead of a sweet eastern box turtle that eats worms and berries and not you, we get a snapping turtle. At least the nine-spotted ladybug is our insect. (She hadn't been seen for 29 years, but is making a comeback on Long Island—and she doesn't snap.)

Go Outside and Play

Snowshoeing

Five Rivers Environmental Center: 56 Game Farm Road, Delmar, 475-0291. Snowshoes can be rented for $3 a pair for use on the grounds of the environmental center. The center features more than 10 miles of hiking trails. It is open Monday through Saturday, 9 a.m. to 4:30 p.m., and Sunday 1 to 4:30 p.m. Cross-country skiing is available as well.

Albany Pine Bush Preserve: New Karner Road, Albany, 456-0655. Around 18 miles of marked trails are waiting for you to explore, or you can take a guided snowshoe walk (snowshoes provided). Call for reservations.

Downhill Skiing

You can find a number of nearby resorts online, including West Mountain, Hunter Mountain, Jiminy Peak, Gore Mountain, and Windham Mountain, but locally:

Maple Ski Ridge: 2725 Mariaville Road, Schenectady, 381-4700. This is a small, family-owned ski slope just off exit 25A, less than five miles from downtown Schenectady. All levels of skiing and snowboarding, as well as lessons, are available. You will enjoy nice views of the hills from the warming/snack-bar lodge.

Cross-Country Skiing

Available for free or for a small fee at most of the public golf courses, including:

Capital Hills: 650 O'Neil Road, Albany, 438-2208.

Schenectady Municipal Golf Course: 400 Oregon Avenue, Schenectady, 382-5155.

Town of Colonie Golf Course: 418 Consaul Road, Schenectady, 374-4181.

Free at the state and local parks, including:

The Crossings: 580 Albany Shaker Road, Colonie, 438-5587.

Dyken Pond Environmental Center: 475 Dyken Pond Road, Cropseyville, 658-2055.

Grafton Lakes State Park: 61 North Long Pond Road, off Route 2 (12 miles east of Troy), Grafton, 279-1155.

John Boyd Thacher State Park: Route 157 (15 miles southwest of Albany, or 1 Hailes Cave Road if you are using your GPS), Voorheesville, 872-1237.

Normanskill Farm Park: Mill Road, Albany. For information, call the city at 434-2489.

Peebles Island State Park: 10 Delaware Avenue, Cohoes, 237-8643.

Cross-country skiing also is allowed on most bike trails.

For a fee:

Oak Hill Farms Cross Country Ski Center: 1206 Oak Hill Road, Esperance, 875-6700. There are more than 30 kilometers of trails on the 500-acre farm, for beginners to experts.

Ice Skating

Empire State Plaza Ice Rink: Albany. Great little rink on the plaza for free skating. Bring your own skates or rent them here.

Frear Park Ice Rink: Frear Park Road, Troy, 266-0023.

Hudson Valley Community College: 629-4850. Public skating is available on Saturday and Sunday.

Knickerbacker Ice Arena: 103rd Street and Eighth Avenue, Lansingburg, 235-7761. Public skating also is offered.

Town of Colonie: The Crossings pond or the Town Hall pond, 785-4301.

Dog Parks

If you live in one of the suburbs surrounding Albany, you probably have your own, resident-only dog park. Delmar, Niskayuna, and Guilderland have very nice off-leash dog parks, but they have yearly fees and residence requirements. Most of the public parks allow any leashed dogs, if you pick up after them. Albany has four very nice off-leash parks, open dawn to dusk, year round. The rules are simple: You have to stay with your dog and clean up after your dog, and if your dog does not play well with others he has to go home.

Department of General Services Off-Lead Area: Erie Boulevard, off Erie Street, north of Huck Finn's Warehouse. This is a nice-sized park with plenty of run room, a gazebo and picnic table, and a drinking fountain for water. If you have tiny dogs, walk the perimeter as there are a couple of spots that a little dog could squirm through.

Normanskill Farm Dog Park: Off Delaware Avenue. Heading toward Delmar, take Mill Road on the left, just before the bridge that goes over the Normanskill. The park is not very well marked, so really watch for Mill Road. Take this road down to the parking area. You have to park in the first parking lot and then walk back to the community gardens and dog park. This is another good-sized park, but no gazebo for you. The (city-owned) farm has miles of trails that your leashed dog is more than welcome to hike with you.

Hartman Road Dog Park: Off New Scotland Road on Hartman Road. The park is almost immediately on your left, next to the community gardens. This is a smaller space, but has a few trees and a couple of places for you to sit. If you blink, you will miss the turnoff for this park, so stay alert!

Westland Hills Dog Park: This is just off Colvin Avenue, behind the Armory car dealership. Look for the sign for the Frank Waterson Park/ Westland Hills Park and you are there. This is a pretty small park. There are no tables; however, it is surrounded by trees, so it looks pretty nice.

Check out the rules for off-season dog walking at municipal golf courses. **Capital Hills** is a good one for Fido in the winter.

Bowling

Del Lanes: 4 Bethlehem Court, Delmar, 439-2224. Very family-friendly alley with bumpers in all lanes for the kids, great deals for school breaks and summer vacation. Bowling alley food and a nice bar for the grownups.

Olympic Lanes: 5 Elmwood Road, off Broadway, Menands, 465-3505. Located very close to Albany, this bowling center has 50 lanes. Been around awhile and has that old-time bowling alley feel to it. Check for open times, as it sometimes closes for the summer.

Playdium Bowling Center: 363 Ontario Street, Albany, 438-0300. Yes, there really is a nice bowling alley near downtown. All the bells and whistles, and beer. The hours change seasonally, so call before you head out.

Spare Time Bowling Center: 375 Troy-Schenectady Road, Latham, 785-6694. If you are out and about and find yourself in Latham, this is a nice alley to stop by.

Sunset Lanes: 1160 Central Avenue, Albany, 438-6404. This clean bowling alley is located in a pretty building and has great pricing and great pizza. Caters to league bowling, so the lanes fill up. The hours change seasonally, so check the website, www.bowlsunset.com, to be sure.

Uncle Sam Lanes: 600 Fulton Street, Troy, 271-7800. This is a neighborhood bowling alley with discount games on certain nights. Cheap snack bar and beer. Really, all you need.

Rock Wall Climbing

A.I.R.: 4C Vatrano Road, Albany, 459-7625. A.I.R features indoor rock climbing and spelunking.

The Edge: 1544 Route 9, Halfmoon, 982-5545. New, bigger than A.I.R., with higher walls, and boulders. Fun for all ages.

Indoor Baseball

AllStars Academy: 198 Troy-Schenectady Road (Route 2), Latham, 220-9140.

Roller Skating

Guptill's Arena: 1085 New Loudon Road (Route 9), Cohoes, 785-0660. This is roller skating at its best, with a beautiful, huge floor. There is nothing else like this around. Bring your own skates or rent here.

Dance and Exercise Classes

The Arts Center of the Capital Region: 265 River Street, Troy, 273-0552. The Arts Center offers classes in belly dancing, ballet, modern dance, yoga, and more. Check out their class listings on their website. www.artcenteronline.org/dance-fitness/

The Center for Nia and Yoga: 4 Central Avenue, Albany, 463-5145. The center offers classes in Nia exercise/dance.

eba: 351 Hudson Avenue (corner of Lark and Hudson), 465-9916. eba has a full lineup of all types of dance classes that you can take. The cost of a semester is amazingly cheap, and it's a great workout besides.

YMCA: Area YMCAs are located in Albany (North Pearl Street), Bethlehem, Clifton Park, Glenville, East Greenbush, Schenectady, Guilderland, and Troy (http://www.cdymca.org/). All YMCAs offer exercise programs.

Skateboarding

Chatham Skatepark: Crellin Park, Route 66, Chatham, 392-0337. Not a big list of outdoor skateparks in the Capital District. This one's not quite complete, but it's useable and free.

Mini-Golf and Fun Parks

Control Tower: 1050 Troy-Schenectady Road, Latham, 782-9242.

Funplex Funpark: 589 Columbia Turnpike, East Greenbush, 477-2651. Mini-golf and so much more.

Pirate's Hideout Inc.: 175 Guideboard Road, Halfmoon, 373-8438. There are no pirates here, but lots of water, and OK ice cream.

Museums

There are a ton of them, including:

The Albany Heritage Area Visitors Center Museum: 25 Quackenbush Square, Albany, 434-0405. Nice museum with a good overview of the city's history, a USS *Albany* exhibit, and the Henry Hudson Planetarium. This museum offers a free orientation film.

Albany Institute of History and Art: 125 Washington Avenue, Albany, 463-4478. The entrance fee is $10 adults, $8 students and seniors, $6 children ages 6 to 12. Entrance is free for Albany's First Friday. This museum offers a great glimpse into Albany's past with great changing exhibits.

Crailo State Historic Site: 9½ Riverside Avenue, Rensselaer, 463-8738. Fort Crailo was built in 1712 by Hendrick Van Rensselaer on the 1,500-acre estate that was part of his grandfather Killian's original patroonship. It had a small fort on the property dating back to the 1600s. Catharine Schuyler (nee Van Rensselaer) was born here. This is where "Yankee Doodle" was written.

Historic Cherry Hill: 523½ South Pearl Street, Albany, 434-4791. Home to the artifacts of the Van Rensselaer-Rankin families. Chock full of history.

Irish American Heritage Museum: 370 Broadway, Albany, 427-1916. Open year round with access to the exhibits, library and other resources.

New York State Museum at Empire State Plaza: 264 Madison Avenue, Albany, 474-5877. This is always a fun experience. It is a large museum containing New York history, artifacts, dioramas of the state's flora and fauna, a life-size Iroquois longhouse, the Cohoes Mastodon—you get the idea. Lots of exhibits.

Schuyler Mansion: 32 Catherine Street, Albany, 434-0834. Home to the Schuyler family (General Philip Schuyler of the Revolutionary War). Lots of family heirlooms; lots of stories here.

Shaker Heritage Museum: 875 Watervliet Shaker Road, Colonie (near the airport), 456-7890. This museum is the oldest Shaker settlement in

America. It is situated on 770 acres with eight of the original buildings, a beautiful herb garden, an orchard, Ann Lee Pond, and the Shaker cemetery. Saturday tours are offered, and special events are held during the year.

Ten Broeck Mansion: 9 Ten Broeck Place, Albany, 436-9826. Cool historic home of the Ten Broeck family. Summer archeological digs in the backyard.

USS *Slater*: Port of Albany, corner of Broadway and Quay Street, Albany, 431-1943. Take a tour on one of the last remaining World War II destroyer escorts. Open April to November.

Go to the Movies

Regal and Bowtie Cinemas are great, but these Albany theaters have something special about them:

The Spectrum 8 Theaters: 290 Delaware Avenue, 449-8995. Downtown has the best theater around, offering a great choice of movies, from art films to blockbusters, 365 days a year. And they have their own parking lots.

The Madison Theater: 1036 Madison Avenue (in Pine Hills), 438-0040. Since Tierra Farm took this place over and completely overhauled it, it's become a great date destination again. Three movie theaters, where you can see second-run blockbusters (who had time to see them the first time round?) for cheap, and a live performance venue. Street parking is pretty available most nights.

The Palace Theatre: 19 Clinton Avenue, 465-3334. Located downtown, this theater has a free summer classic movie program that can be found on its website, www.palacealbany.com.

Go to the Theater

There is great local theater all over the Capital District. Check their websites or the *Times Union Preview* section for listings.

Albany Civic Theater: 235 Second Avenue, Albany, 462-1297.

Circle Theater Players: 2880 Route 43, Averill Park, 674-2007.

Capital Repertory Theatre: 111 North Pearl Street, Albany, 445-7469.

Classic Theater Guild: At Proctors, 137 State Street, Schenectady, 387-9150. Free summer shows in the Helderbergs at Indian Ladder Farm.

Cohoes Music Hall: 58 Remsen Street, Cohoes, 237-5858. Focus is on kids' productions and classes.

Curtain Call Theatre: 210 Old Loudon Road, Latham, 877-7529.

Ghent Playhouse: 6 Town Hall Place, Ghent, 392-6264. Excellent in every way.

Mopco (The Mop and Bucket Company): 309 Union Street, Schenectady, 248-7430, www.mopco.org. Improv theater.

Park Playhouse: Shows at the Lakehouse in Albany's Washington Park, 434-0776.

RPI Players: 110 Eighth Street, on the RPI campus, Troy, 276-6503.

Schenectady Civic Players: 12 South Church Street, Schenectady, 382-2081.

Schenectady Light Opera Company (SLOC): 427 Franklin Street, Schenectady, 350-7378.

Spotlight Players: spotlightplayersny@gmail.com. Spotlight Players do not have their own performance space, so the venue can change. Great shows usually in East Greenbush at Columbia High School.

Steamer 10 Theatre: 500 Western Avenue, 438-5503.

The Theater Barn: 654 Route 20, New Lebanon, 794-8989.

Troy Civic Theatre: www.troycivic.org. Relatively new company with some outstanding productions under their belt. Think about supporting them so they can continue bringing wonderful, affordable theater to the Capital Region.

Art and Other Types of Classes

Albany Art Room: 350 New Scotland Avenue, Albany, 966-2781. Classes in drawing, printmaking, cartooning, and bookmaking for adults and children are offered at convenient times. There is a store on-site where you can buy supplies, so it is easy for you to get started on your creative path. Visit albanyartroom.com for a full lineup of classes and times.

Arts Center of the Capital Region: 265 River Street, Troy, 273-0552. The Arts Center offers classes in drawing, jewelry making, printmaking, stained glass, and a number of others, including yoga and belly dancing. Visit www.artscenteronline.org for more information.

Broken Mold Studio: 284 River Street, Troy, 273-6041. Pottery-making classes are offered for all ages. Go and get your hands dirty.

Planetariums and Stargazing

Albany Area Amateur Astronomers, Inc.: Meetings are on the third Thursday of each month at miSci, and in August they host their George Landis Arboretum and Grafton Lakes Star Parties to share information and gaze upon the heavens. You are welcome to join them. For a schedule of dates, visit dudleyobservatory.org/AAAA/star-party-schedule/.

Henry Hudson Planetarium at the Albany Visitors Center: 25 Quackenbush Square, Albany, 434-0405. Planetarium shows are held on the third Saturday of each month at 11 a.m. and 1 p.m. The earlier show is more kid-friendly. Show prices are only $3.

Hirsch Observatory: RPI campus, Troy, 423-3510. The Hirsch Observatory is open to the public on Saturday nights from February to mid-November, 8 to 10 p.m. From the observatory you can peer into the universe, right from Troy. There is parking on the street, as well as in the College Avenue parking lot. If it's cloudy, astronomy programs are held in Room 2C30 of the Science Center.

miSci Planetarium: 15 Nott Terrace Heights, Schenectady, 382-7890. Shows are on Saturdays at 1, 2, and 3 p.m., and Tuesday through Friday at 2 p.m. They have ticket combos for the museum too.

Take a Tour

Capitol Tours: These tours of the New York State Capitol building are free and are offered Monday through Saturday. Check the website for times.

Captain JP Cruise Line: 278 River Street, Troy, 270-1901. We always have fun on a Captain JP cruise. The food is excellent, the music is great, and the view along the Hudson is always beautiful. Their boats can carry up to 600 passengers, making the cruise more of an event than a tour.

Dutch Apple Cruises: Located at the Snow Dock at the Port of Albany, boarding at Madison Avenue and Broadway, 463-0220. A variety of cruises on the beautiful Hudson River are offered. Visit www.dutchapplecruises. com for descriptions and dates. These are seasonal cruises.

Walking Tours: Maps for these tours can be found at the Albany and Schenectady visitors centers. The historical societies also have scheduled walking tours during the year. The Albany Visitors Center has its own free guided walking tour in good weather, so check for dates or call 434-0405.

Art Galleries

Albany International Airport Gallery: Third floor at the airport, 242-2241. Yes, the airport. This 2,500-square-foot space holds a couple of wonderfully curated exhibits every year. The gallery is open from 7 a.m. to 11 p.m. every day and is *free!* It is well worth the visit, and you can watch the planes take off next to the gallery.

Esther Massry Gallery at the Massry Center for the Arts: 1002 Madison Avenue, Albany, 485-3902. This relatively new facility on the College of Saint Rose campus features outstanding art and lectures from visual artists from around the world as well as the impressive work of students and faculty.

The Foundry for Art Design + Culture: 119 Remsen Street, Cohoes, 229-2173. As well as offering unique art services to the community, the Foundry has a gallery space that hosts some really outstanding artists.

Mandeville Gallery: 807 Union Street, Schenectady, 388-6000. Located on the second floor of the beautiful Nott Memorial on the Union College campus, the gallery hosts new exhibits about three times a year.

Opalka Gallery, Sage College of Albany: 140 New Scotland Avenue, Albany, 292-7742. A beautiful exhibit space that showcases faculty and student artwork.

New York State Museum Galleries: 264 Madison Avenue, Albany, 474-5877. The changing shows in the many galleries in the museum offer you a chance to see different art from around the country and around the world. Some pretty amazing shows have passed through Albany in the last couple of years. It's a bargain to boot.

Music to Your Ears

You can find live music everywhere. Albany, Troy, and Schenectady all have free summer music series, and depending on what you prefer, local bars, small music venues, and some of the local college campuses offer a wide variety of music any night of the week. The *Times Union* Thursday *Preview* section provides an overwhelming now-and-later rundown of who's performing where. Here are the big and fairly big ones for national acts:

The Egg: Empire State Plaza, Albany, 473-1845, www.theegg.org. Two terrific stages, great acts.

EMPAC at RPI: 110 8th Street, Troy, 276-3921. EMPAC features experimental (and we mean experimental) music, theater, and dance. Visit the website at empac.rpi.edu.

Massry Center for the Arts at the College of St. Rose: 1002 Madison Avenue, Albany, 337-4871. This arts center also has a performance space. Visit www.strose.edu/massry.

Palace Theatre: 19 Clinton Avenue, Albany, www.palacealbany.com.

Proctors: 432 State Street, Schenectady, 346-6204, www.proctors.org.

The Times Union Center: 51 South Pearl Street, Albany, 487-2000, timesunioncenter-albany.com.

The Troy Savings Bank Music Hall: 30 2nd Street, Troy, 273-0038, www.troymusichall.org.

Upstate Concert Hall: 1208 Route 146, Clifton Park, 371-0012, upstateconcerthall.com.

Local colleges, including RPI and UAlbany, also sponsor bigger acts in their sports arenas. Check their calendars online.

Some of the smaller places, as well as clubs and bars around town, that feature music include:

The Ale House: 680 River Street, Troy, 272-9740. Great food *and* great music (national and local). One of the best. Really.

The Hollow Bar & Kitchen: 79 North Pearl Street, Albany, 462-9033. Terrific place for hearing national/international and local bands, plus food.

The Linda (WAMC): 339 Central Avenue, Albany, 465-5233.

The Low Beat: 335 Central Avenue, Albany, 432-6572. One of the best around, and, once a month, a killer Rock N Roll Brunch you'll have to wait in line for.

McGeary's Pub: 4 Clinton Square, Albany, 463-1455. Check the pub's online calendar for bands.

The Moon and River Café: 115 South Ferry Street, Schenectady, 382-1938. Tiny place with one of the best open mics around.

Parish Public House: 388 Broadway, Albany, 465-0444. Featuring a live music venue and a Cajun menu, Parish Public House is located across from the D&H/SUNY Plaza building.

Open Mics

There are dozens of these around town. The best source online is CapitalRegionOpenMics on Facebook. Here are a few of the ones we like:

Arts Center of the Capital Region: 265 River Street, Troy, 273-0552. Hosts an open mic once a month in the Joseph Bruno Theater.

The Daily Grind: 46 3rd Street, Troy, 272-8658. Open mic on Troy Night Out (last Friday of the month), 6–9 p.m.

Emack and Bolio's: 366 Delaware Avenue, Albany, 512-5100. Open mic Tuesdays.

Hudson River Coffee House: 227 Quail Street, Albany, 449-2174. Open mic Thursday.

The Lark Tavern: 435 Madison Avenue, Albany, 694-8490. Comedy night on Monday.

The Low Beat: 335 Central Avenue, 432-6572. Comedy night Tuesday.

McGeary's: 4 Clinton Square, Albany, 463-1455. Open mic Wednesday.

Moon and River Café: 115 South Ferry Street, Schenectady, 382-1938. Open mic Sunday.

Rustic Barn Pub: 150 Speigletown Road, Troy, 235-5858. Open mic Thursday.

Especially for the Kids

Adirondack Animal Land: 3554 New York Route 30, Gloversville, 883-5748. Little kids love this place, lots to look at, lots of animals to pet, and a cool little drive through African safari. They have a cafe, but you can bring a picnic lunch. Open May-September.

Albany Pine Bush Discovery Center: 195 New Karner Road, Albany, 456-0655. This center introduces you to the Pine Bush by showing just what makes this ecosystem so special. A few hands-on displays inside, but pick up the map and walk the trails to see it for yourself.

Berkshire Bird Paradise Sanctuary and Botanical Gardens: 43 Red Pond Road, Petersburg, 279-3801. Peter Durbacher has been running this sanctuary since 1975, caring for injured birds from across the country. Eagles, falcons, owls, and even unwanted chickens and wounded pigeons have made their home here. Those that can be rehabilitated are released, but those who cannot survive in the wild are given a loving home for the rest of their lives. All types of animals can be found here, even four-legged ones. There are even greenhouses where tropical plants are grown. The Durbachers run the sanctuary on donations and hard work alone. This is well worth the trip. The sanctuary is open from mid-May to October. Visit www.birdparadise.org for more information and directions.

Children's Museum of Science and Technology: 250 Jordan Road, Troy (in the Rensselaer Tech Park), 235-2120. Hands-on science exhibits, live exotic animals, and changing shows in the dome planetarium theater are the highlights here. You must be accompanied by a child to visit here. No, really.

Five Rivers Environmental Education Center: 56 Game Farm Road, Delmar, 475-0291. Run by the New York State Department of Environmental Conservation, this 446-acre preserve offers 12 miles of trails winding through a diverse number of habitats. There are 16 ponds, fields, orchards, and woods supporting hundreds of species of birds, mammals, and creepy crawly things. The biggest bullfrog we ever saw was in one of the ponds here. There even is an information center with exhibits and bathrooms.

Henry Hudson Planetarium at the Albany Visitors Center: 25 Quackenbush Square, Albany, 434-0405. There are two shows on the third Saturday of each month (11 a.m. and 1 p.m.). The morning show is geared for kids age 6 and under. Learn about the stars with interactive fun for only $3 per person.

Huck Finn's Playland: 25 Erie Boulevard, Albany, 242-7575. After Hoffmans's Playland in Latham closed, Huck Finn's Warehouse moved the whole shebang to Albany, saving one of the greatest kids' amusement parks ever.

miSci Museum and Planetarium: 15 Nott Terrace Heights, Schenectady, 382-7890. This museum focuses on the scientific innovations that came out of this area. The planetarium has shows Tuesday through Saturday.

New York State Museum: 264 Madison Avenue, across from the Empire State Plaza, Albany, 474-5877. This is a large museum containing New York history, artifacts, wildlife, and so on. The Cohoes mastodon is here, as is a working carousel from the early 1900s. Outstanding art exhibits can be viewed in the downstairs galleries. New exhibits are provided every year. The museum is open from 9:30 a.m. to 5 p.m. daily.

Bar Districts

In Albany: Downtown around Pearl, Broadway, State, and Clinton you'll find **The Hollow** (79 North Pearl Street), **Albany Pump Station** (19 Quackenbush Square), **Blue 82** (82 North Pearl Street), **McGeary's** (4 Clinton Square), the **Barrel Saloon** (942 Broadway), **Druthers** (1053 Broadway), the **Merry Monk** (90 North Pearl Street), the **Olde English Pub** (25 Quackenbush Square), **Parish Public House** (388 Broadway), and **City Beer Hall** (42 Howard Street). All fine establishments; and there are many more, so look around. Smaller, more intimate bars can be found in the Lark Street and Madison Avenue area, including **Bombers** (258 Lark Street), **Café Hollywood** (275 Lark Street), the **Lionheart Pub** (448 Madison Avenue), **Lark Tavern** (453 Madison Avenue, and **Oh Bar** (304 Lark Street). College bars are found west of downtown along Madison Avenue, Western Avenue, Central Avenue and New Scotland Avenue, including the **Ginger Man** (234 Western Avenue), **Pauly's Hotel** (337 Central Avenue), **Tierra Coffee Roasters** (1038 Madison Avenue), and **The Pub** (869 Madison Avenue). Madison Avenue rounds out its bar district with **The Point** (1100 Madison—nice bar but nicer than pub fare restaurant) and the **Madison Pour House** (1110 Madison Avenue—wonderful beer selection and delicious food in a really comfortable setting).

In Troy: River Street north of the Green Island Bridge has a small row of very nice pubs, including **Browns Brewing Co.** (417–19 River Street) and **Wolf's Biergarten** (2 King Street). Farther north on River Street is a Trojan favorite, the **Ale House** (680 River Street). **Lucas Confectionery** (12 2nd Street), **Tavern Bar** (upstairs from Peck's Arcade, 217 Broadway), **Finnbar's Pub** (452 Broadway), **Bootleggers on Broadway** (200 Broadway), **Footsy Magoos** (17 1st Street), the **Ruck**

(104 3rd Street), and many more excellent establishments are located throughout downtown Troy, which is not that big, so you can walk between them.

In Schenectady: Try **Ambition Café** on Jay Street, **Bombers** and **Mexican Radio** on State, the **Van Dyke, Manhattan Exchange**, and **Union Inn**, all on Union Street, and for your Irish pubs, try **Pinhead Susan's** on North Broadway and **Katie O'Byrne's** on Wall Street.

> **Note:** Most of our restaurants listed also have very nice bar offerings to go along with your meals.

Friday Arts Nights

Held in downtown Troy, Albany, and Schenectady; you can enjoy art, music, and shopping.

Albany's First Friday: First Friday of the month.

Troy Night Out: Last Friday of the month.

Art Night Schenectady: Third Friday of every month.

Things You Shouldn't Do but Will

Body Modification

The Dead Presidents Lounge: 5 South Allen Street, Albany, 689-0730. Terrific work.

Impulse Tattoo: 365 Feura Bush Road, Glenmont, 427-1000. Great art; check their online gallery.

Lark Tattoo: 278 Lark Street, Albany, 432-1905. Great work in a friendly downtown location.

After your tattoo you can go get something pierced at:

Lark Vegas Piercing Co.: 273 Lark Street, Albany, 434-4907. For all your piercing needs.

Tom Spaulding Tattoo Studio: 628 Central Avenue, Albany, 482-6477. This has been a fixture on Central since 1978, and has some of the best artists around.

Let's Eat!

In Albany

Albany Pump Station: 19 Quackenbush Square, Albany, 447-9000. This historic pump station built in the 1870s is now the home of C.H. Evans Brewery and the Albany Pump Station restaurant. Big menu of great food, big menu of great beer, all in a really comfortable setting. Lots of parking. Lunch (which is terrific) and dinner.

Angelo's 677 Prime: 677 Broadway, Albany, 427-7463. Angelo's is a superior, very upscale steakhouse. Have your rich aunt take you here for a meal to remember.

Bombers Burrito Bar: 258 Lark Street, Albany, 935-1098. This is Albany's landmark burrito bar, and now it's a Schenectady one, too (447 State Street, 374-3548). Delicious burritos the size of babies, wings, cheese fries, etc., and a full bar.

Buffalo Wagon: 6 Metro Park Road, Albany, 689-0937. This is in one of those strip malls off Wolf Road, so you'd never find it if you weren't looking for it. Pan-Asian cuisine and sushi. We enjoy everything we order here. The portions are large, and unlike some other Chinese food places, when you reheat the leftovers, they are still good. The ingredients are all top quality and it tastes like it. You can order to go, but their wait staff is so friendly, it's a pleasure to dine in.

Café Capriccio: 49 Grand Street, Albany, 465-0439. *Metroland* named this Albany's best restaurant at least a dozen times. The gourmet Italian cuisine is phenomenal, and the owner and staff make sure your dining experience is perfect. Housed in a great old brownstone that was once part of Albany's old Italian neighborhood, it has a great bygone feel to it. Open for dinner; parking across the street.

Caffe Italia: 662 Central Avenue, Albany, 459-8029. This is one of those small, family-run Italian restaurants with some of the best food around. Fabulous sauces, crisp salads, nothing disappoints. It has limited seating, so make reservations. You'll be back.

Café Madison: 1108 Madison Avenue, Albany, 935-1094. This will be your favorite café. Stop in for a fabulous breakfast and come back for lunch.You'll have to wait for breakfast/brunch on weekends, so plan on some extra time. You won't be disappointed.

Café 217: 12½ Delaware Avenue, Albany, 462-0050. Definitely fills a niche for those hungry night owls in the wee weekend hours. Great breakfast menu. Open Wednesday and Thursday 5–11 p.m., and from 5 p.m. Friday straight through to 3 p.m. Sunday.

Capital Q Smokehouse: 329 Ontario Street, Albany, 438-7675. One of the best BBQ places in the area—pulled pork, ribs, tremendous brisket, and a pretty good choice of sides. The place has basically no seating, so this is an order-online-and-pick-it-up place.

Capital Thai: 997 Central Avenue, Albany, 489-4840. When you really crave authentic Thai food, come here. All the wonderful spices and dishes you want, for lunch or dinner.

The Cheese Traveler: 540 Delaware Avenue, Albany, 443-0440. We love cheese. More than anything else, except maybe chocolate. You can buy all kinds of cheeses you've never had before, eat grilled cheese sandwiches on fresh, local bread, and enjoy homemade soups for lunch or an early dinner. You can add fresh meats to your sandwich which is topped off with a fresh pickle. And they have poutine!! Did we mention that?!

The Daily Grind: 204 Lark Street, Albany, 434-1482. This is the cozy (small) downtown Albany coffee shop. It serves sandwiches, soups, desserts, and coffee like the Troy one, just in a smaller setting.

El Loco Mexican Café: 465 Madison Avenue, Albany, 436-1855. El Loco's version of Tex-Mex. The food is good and reasonably priced. They've been here a really long time and know what they're doing.

El Mariachi: 289 Hamilton Street, Albany, 432-7580. Good Mexican food is served in a friendly, comfortable setting. You can enjoy the lively downstairs patio or go upstairs for a quiet dinner.

French Press Café & Creperie: 5 Clinton Square, Albany, 275-0478. If you are looking for out-of-this-world crepes, sweets, and sandwiches, here's your place. Right across from the Palace Theatre. Amazing choices; all delicious.

The Gateway Diner: 899 Central Avenue, Albany, 482-7557. Serving really good breakfasts, lunches, and dinners, the Gateway has a full menu, a great diner feel, and the friendliest wait staff.

The Ginger Man: 234 Western Avenue, Albany, 427-5963. Known for its truly extensive wine list, the Ginger Man also offers a large variety of delicious comfort foods with some interesting twists. Definitely worth a try if you've never been here before.

Hidden Café: Delaware Plaza, 180 Delaware Avenue, Delmar, 439-8800. Hidden off to the side in the shopping plaza, this place is worth looking for. The Mediterranean offerings, including falafel, kabobs, and more unusual entrees, are consistently delicious. They can also cater your private parties.

Ichiban: 338 Central Avenue, Albany, 432-0358. We have always enjoyed the food here, especially their orange tofu and sushi. Eat in or take out.

Iron Gate Café: 182 Washington Avenue, Albany, 445-3555. Great sandwiches at great prices. One of the best places in town to get lunch. They also have a terrific breakfast and brunch menu. Open 8–3.

Jack's Oyster House: 42 State Street, Albany, 465-8854. Opened in 1913, Jack's is part of Albany's history and continues to serve excellent seafood and steak in its downtown restaurant.

Karavalli: 9B Johnson Road, Latham, 785-7600. This place has some of the best Indian food in the area. Excellent lunch buffet and dinner.

La Empanada Llama: 469 Delaware Avenue, Albany, 915-1887. Peruvian. Easy place to stop for a quick bite before a movie at the Spectrum. Lots of choices. No time? Try them out at the Schenectady Greenmarket on Sundays.

Latham 76 Diner: 722 New Loudon Road, Latham, 785-3793. This diner has a couple of things going for it. First, it's open 365 days a year! Second, it is open 24 hours! The food and service are excellent as well, but this place has been a sanctuary for those who just need a quiet place to drink a cup of coffee when everyone else is sleeping.

La Serre: 14 Green Street, Albany, 463-6056. Lovely, genteel setting for excellent Italian pasta and French entrees. They serve a French onion soup exactly as it should be.

Mamoun's Restaurant: 206 Washington Avenue, Albany, 434-3901. Mediterranean cuisine with outstanding pitas and falafel. Open every day for your falafel fix. Mmmmmm.

McGeary's Pub: 4 Clinton Square, Albany, 463-1455. A friendly Irish pub, McGeary's serves amazing appetizers.

Milano: 594 New Loudon Road (Newton Plaza), Latham, 783-3334. Quality northern Italian cuisine, pizzas, great appetizers, nice bar. . . . We have never had a bad meal here, small or larger group. Nice staff; comfortable restaurant.

New World Bistro Bar: 300 Delaware Avenue (near the Spectrum 8 Theatres), Albany, 694-0520. Creatively prepared, with fresh, local ingredients, the meals here are superb. Open for dinner every day and brunch on Sundays. Check their menu online so you can think about what you would love to eat. Get here early or make a reservation because it gets tight.

The Orchard Tavern: 68 North Manning Boulevard, Albany, 482-5677. Since 1903, this has been an Albany tradition. Their own style of pizza with their original delicious sauce, and great choices for lunch or dinner. Nice bar selection, too.

Pho Yum: 272 Delaware Avenue, Albany, 465-8899. In the restaurant formerly known as My Linh, the owners have gone with a more casual dining experience, maintaining some of the delicious Vietnamese dishes they were known for.

Professor Java's Coffee Sanctuary: 217 Wolf Road, Colonie, 435-0843. This is one of the most comfortable coffeehouses to hang out in. It serves great coffee, great food, and a big selection of loose teas, and has a great atmosphere. Their desserts are worth saving room for.

Provence: Stuyvesant Plaza, 1475 Western Avenue, Guilderland, 689-7777. We've had good service and mediocre service here, but always good French-American food. We like the piano and the elegant setting.

Riverfront Bar and Grill: 51 Erie Boulevard, in the Corning Preserve, Albany, 426-4738. Enjoy casual dining aboard this barge as you watch the boats go by. There is a full music lineup all summer. Open seasonally for lunch and dinner.

Sam's Italian American Restaurant: 125 Southern Boulevard, Albany, 463-3433. A great family-style Italian restaurant with delicious choices and friendly service. Terrific.

Sitar: 1929 Central Avenue, Albany, 952-2919. Sitar features classic and delicious Indian dining.

Sukhothai: 254 Lark Street, Albany, 463-0223; 62 Central Avenue, Albany, 433-7203. If you crave the flavorings of authentic Thai food, this is where to get it. There are numerous vegetarian choices, and it is reasonably priced.

Tailored Tea: 1010 Troy-Schenectady Road, Latham, 608-5137. It's a very cute little brunch, lunch, and tea place living inside the oldest farmhouse in the Town of Colonie, built by Ebenezer Hills Jr. in 1785. The land was bought by the airport and the house went to ruin until it was declared a historic landmark. The airport then rehabbed it, moved it out of the way of airplanes, and rented it out. Very cool place to visit, and you can have your event here as well.

Taiwan Noodle: 218 Central Avenue, Albany, 436-1328. Perfect. Authentic Chinese noodle dishes, soups, and sides. All at unbelievably low prices.

Tanpopo Ramen and Sake Bar: 893 Broadway (the old Miss Albany Diner), Albany, 451-9868. Really, a perfect addition to the warehouse district. Open for lunch and dinner.

Terra International Cuisine and NuWave Café & Bar: 238 Washington Avenue, Albany, 463-5600. A delightful combo of raw-vegetable and bar café welcomes you with a full-service dining room behind it. Both are closed Mondays; Terra closes for Friday nights. The menu is kosher, vegetarian, vegan, and a bit Indian. The food is simply superb.

Tierra Coffee Roasters: 1038 Madison Avenue, Albany, 621-7299. Great improvement over the Muddy Cup, which used to be here. They serve a healthy, but still delicious, breakfast, lunch, and lunch-supper with vegetarian and vegan options. Their own coffee is excellent, but their bar also serves a good selection of beers and wine. They are right next to the Madison Theater, which they own, and have completely overhauled, making it a great destination again.

Van's Vietnamese Restaurant: 307 Central Avenue, Albany, 436-1868. Van's is an outstanding Vietnamese restaurant where everything is delicious, especially the spring rolls.

Wolff's Biergarten: 895 Broadway, Albany, 427-2461. You can get all kinds of wursts here to go with all kinds of German and Belgian beer. Sit at a picnic table to enjoy them. Fun, casual setting. Like having a picnic indoors.

Yono's: 25 Chapel Street, Albany (located in the Hampton Inn). Yono's provides comfortable elegance and the absolute best Indonesian and continental dishes, beautifully presented. You will not be disappointed. Open for dinner only. Closed Sundays.

In Troy

The Ale House: 680 River Street, Troy, 272-9740. This is a great place for traditional, soul-enriching pub food. Check their calendar for the outstanding musical lineup. Open for lunch and dinner.

Ali Baba: 2243 15th Street, Troy, 273-1170. Serving Turkish fare. *Everything* is delicious. We could eat their lavash bread hot from the oven all day long, but then there wouldn't be room for anything else, like kebobs, wraps, pide, or their specialty salads. Service is great.

Beirut: 184 River Street, Troy, 270-9404. A little Lebanese place with lots of tasty choices and wonderful falafel.

The Brown Bag: 156 4th Street, Troy, 279-7699. Open 5 p.m. to the wee hours. Made-to-order burgers, fries, veggies, homemade ice cream sandwiches, and cookies. Not a fast-food place; everything is cooked for you, but you can call it in and get it delivered nearby.

Brown's Brewing Company: 417 River Street, Troy, 273-2337. Excellent pub fare, excellent award-winning craft beer, and a great view of the river. One of the original brew pubs, and definitely one of the best.

Bruegger's Bagels: 55 Congress Street, Troy, 274-4469. For a light breakfast or lunch, Bruegger's has the best bagels on earth, and this store is where it all started.

Cafe Deli-icious: 413 River Street, Troy, 271-8787. Yummy breakfast choices and wonderful sandwiches. They can cater your event for you or create a beautiful gift basket, fancy fruit platter, or a mountain of beautiful specialty chocolates.

The Daily Grind: 46 3rd Street, Troy, 272-8658. This is a homey coffee place with good soups, sandwiches, and baked goods with friendly service. It provides comfortable and relaxing seating areas and a great open mic on the last Friday of every month (Troy Night Out).

DeFazio's Pizzeria: 266 4th Street, Troy, 271-1111. This is where to get that wood-fired pizza you have been craving. There are 21 gourmet varieties, all so good you won't be able to resist eating a slice before you get back to your car. The four-cheese is sublime. Not in the mood for pizza? Try one of their 20 pasta dishes or maybe a calzone with a side of antipasto. They will be moving to new, bigger digs just up the street in the old Vanilla Bean factory. More seating, bigger deli, more of everything we love here. You can eat in, take out, or have it delivered.

Dinosaur Bar-B-Que: 377 River Street, Troy, 309-0400. Great BBQ, great sides, great view, great bar, great fun.

Duncan's Dairy Bar: 890 Hoosick Road, Troy, 279-9985. We asked the waitress how long Duncan's has been here, and she said since the dinosaurs roamed the earth. Some of the décor may date back that far, but it's hard to find such great, fresh, local food anywhere else. The wait staff is delightful, and the chocolate shakes are the best in the area. You can get breakfast, lunch, or dinner every day.

Famous Lunch: 111 Congress Street, Troy, 272-9481. This Troy landmark has been around since 1932, serving little hot dogs smothered in what is called "Zippy" sauce. We'll let you figure out what that is. Named one of the top 75 places in America for hot dogs by Daily Meal in 2015. You need to stop by for a plateful.

Finnbar's Pub: 452 Broadway, Troy, 326-3994 (where Holmes and Watson was). The corner of Broadway and Williams has been home to some pub or another for 100 years. This one is a keeper. Superior pub food at hard-to-beat prices, and an outstanding beer selection. Here's to another 100 years.

Gus's Hot Dogs: 212 25th Street, Watervliet, 273-8743. Since the 1950s, Gus's has been serving up these little hot dogs with a special meat sauce.

This is a tiny, tiny place with a couple of picnic tables outside. The menu consists of hot dogs, hamburgers, and sausage sandwiches. You can get stuffed for under $5.

Illium Café: 9 Broadway, Troy, 273-7700. Yes, they spell it wrong. Drives us nuts, but the food is good and inexpensive. We've always liked the comfortable feel of the place, good for breakfast, brunch, lunch, or a very early dinner. They are closed in the evening except for the last Friday of the month (Troy Night Out).

Infinity Café: 172 River Street, Troy, 491-5657. Another great place to get some delicious, fresh homemade food. Open for breakfast and lunch. Amazing pancakes, sandwiches, soups, and more. If you can't get down here during the week, stop in after the farmer's market on Saturday.

Lo Porto Ristorante Caffe: 85 4th Street, Troy, 273-8546. The food is amazing and abundant. We love it here. Lunch is a great deal, but for the amount of food you get for dinner, the prices are more than reasonable. The calamari appetizer is enough to feed a small country. This is not a big place, so reservations are a good idea.

Manory's Restaurant: 99 Congress Street, Troy, 266-9300. Manory's has been in business at this location since 1913, which says they are doing something right. Stop in for satisfying diner-type fare or an anytime hearty breakfast.

Muza: 1300 15th Street (near Congress), Troy, 271-6892. Excellent family-style Polish/Eastern European cuisine. When we were deciding what to order, the waitress told us that we really wanted stuffed cabbage, and she was right.

Peck's Arcade: 217 Broadway, Troy, 326-3450; **Lucas Confectionary:** 12 2nd Street, Troy, 326-3450; the **Grocery:** 211 Broadway, Troy, 326-3450; and the **Tavern Bar:** upstairs from Peck's. We put these all together because they are. Lucas Confectionary is a terrific wine bar with some really great plates of goodies. Peck's offers small-plate dishes of inspired cooking, with great vegetable plates as well as unusual palate-pleasing meat dishes. You can spend a lot, or just start with a few plates to see how good everything is. The Tavern Bar upstairs is a small bar with a knack for creating memorable cocktails. Just want a great sandwich or take-home cheese and meat? The Grocery is there for you. They all share a delightful covered, interior patio, which is great for parties or events or to just enjoy. Each name reflects its former incarnation. The owners have really made their establishments great Troy destinations.

Pig Pit BBQ: 1 Niver Street, Cohoes, 235-2323. A local favorite. Great pulled pork sandwiches, some really nice sides prepared right, Tex-Mex, eat in or take out.

Placid Baker: 250 Broadway, Troy, 326-2657. We love their bread and hermit cookies, and they make great, healthy soups and sandwiches for lunch, which are delicious. They are regulars at the Troy Waterfront Farmer's Market, so you can catch them there as well.

Plum Blossom: 685 Hoosick Road, Troy, 272-0036. This is where we bring our visiting friends for excellent Chinese food. Everything is good. The décor is amazing.

River Street Café: 429 River Street, Troy, 273-2740. Delicious fresh food is served in a beautiful setting with a great view of the river. Excellent wine list. This is one of our favorites for a special night out.

The Rusty Anchor: 1 Selke Drive, Hudson Shores Park, Watervliet, 273-2920. Right across from Troy, this is comfortable barge dining with a beautiful view of the Hudson, with live music every weekend during the summer.

Shalimar: 407 Fulton Street, Troy, 273-8744. Delicious Indian fare with a very nice lunch buffet at a good price.

The Shop: 135 4th Street, Troy, 874-1899. We were big fans of Trojan Hardware and loved to snake our way through 90 years of plumbing parts in their catacombs. When it closed, we were sad to see another piece of Troy history gone, but no! The Shop has incorporated the soul of it with its unique, industrial/hardware décor that we just love. The restaurant/bar offers tasty, eclectic dishes and a good selection of local craft beers and alcohols. Not in the mood for dinner? Come for an excellent brunch.

Slidin' Dirty: 9 1st Street, Troy, 326-8492. If you're a fan of their food truck, you will love the brick-and-mortar location even more. The restaurant is housed in the old Wm. H. Young book bindery, and you can now order everything on the menu at once and eat it off real plates. Try their delicious mac-and-cheese balls, or any one of their traditional or exotic sliders. They have a full bar as well.

Spill'n the Beans: 13 3rd Street, Troy, 268-1028. With a large selection of coffee, eclectic breakfast and lunch selections, and better-than-most pastries, this place has an extremely comfortable lounge area with a fireplace (Wi-Fi, too) so you can really sit and enjoy your coffee.

Sweet Sue's: 203 River Street, Troy, 892-2933. An absolute gem of a place making delicious brunch/lunch meals from local ingredients. And the desserts! Check them out at the Troy farmer's market or stop by the shop.

Ted's Fish Fry: 447 3rd Avenue, Watervliet; 203 Wolf Road, Albany; 636 New Loudon Road, Latham. Local chain with the best fish fry around. We go to the Watervliet one all the time. Love it.

Troy Kitchen: 77 Congress Street, Troy. New to Troy, located in the old Pioneer grocery store, is a really cool, sort-of food court. Multiple vendors selling from their own tiny kitchens. We were happy to find excellent Korean food at K-Plate (limited choices but good and cheap), crepes at La Petite Crepe, Mexican food at Magdalena's, and real Maine lobster rolls from Troy Lobster. They have a large sweets and desserts counter where you can get coffee as well. The space is large and open with a very nice performance area that has a beer and wine bar for its evening patrons. Music, poetry some evenings.

In Schenectady

Ambition Café: 154 Jay Street, Schenectady, 382-9277. You can get a great sandwich for lunch or dinner here, along with offerings from their full bar. The café features a funky atmosphere with some great kitschy art covering the walls.

Aperitivo Bistro: 426 State Street, Schenectady, 579-3371. Busy place when Proctors has a show, so expect an abbreviated menu. Other times, just relax and enjoy your choice of good Italian, American, unusual pizza selections, and more from a very appetizing menu. They have a full bar with a decent selection. We've heard mixed reviews from people we don't know, but our friends love this place.

The Appian Way: 1839 Van Vranken Avenue, Schenectady, 393-8460. Not your Olive Garden-variety Italian food. This is the real deal. Fresh everything, made for you when you order. The menu may sound basic, but the flavors are anything but. Really good food prepared by really good cooks. There will be a wait, but you know what they say about good things. And these are even better.

Blue Ribbon Restaurant: 1801 State Street, Schenectady, 393-2600. One of the Capital Region's best. Big menu with lots of great choices. Greek, Italian, everything else, all good. Friendly staff, fabulous desserts. You can't go wrong here.

Canali's Restaurant: 126 Mariaville Road, Schenectady, 355-5323. If you're looking for one of those great Italian restaurants with enormous portions of food so delicious you won't mind eating the leftovers for days, then Canali's is for you. Busy, friendly place. You can make reservations, but you can also order to go. Just as delicious.

Cornell's Restaurant: 39 North Jay Street, Schenectady, 370-3825. Cornell's has been located in Schenectady's Little Italy since 1943, and serves up an outstanding menu your Italian grandmother would be jealous of. Go, eat.

Ferrari's Ristorante: 1254 Congress Street, Schenectady, 382-8865. Another great family Italian restaurant. Heaping portions of your favorites in a simple setting surrounded by happy people. What could be better?

Gershon's Deli & Caterers: 1600 Union Street, Schenectady, 393-0617. A mainstay on Union forever, this is one of the best delis around. Fresh, delicious meats and cheeses, fabulous sandwiches and sides. You really can't go wrong here. You can even pick up a loaf of Perreca's wonderful bread here.

Glen Sanders Mansion: 1 Glen Avenue, Scotia, 374-7262. Angelo's Tavolo (Mazzone Hospitality) is where to have an elegant and deliciously satisfying dinner in one of the truly historic homes in the Capital District. The view of the Mohawk is spectacular. Italian specialties, but everything they prepare is done with perfection.

Jumpin' Jacks Drive-In: 5 Schonowee Avenue, Scotia (right over the bridge from Schenectady), 393-6101. A sure sign of spring is the opening day and long line at Jumpin' Jacks. This is a seasonal place that has been around forever, serving up great fast food (especially the onion rings) and creamy soft-serve ice cream that you can eat overlooking the beautiful Mohawk River. The US Water Ski Show Team has its home just behind Jack's (Jack's has been a proud sponsor of the ski team for over 25 years), and you can watch them practice while eating your ice cream. Google US Water Ski Show Team for their showtimes (usually Tuesdays at 6:30 or 7 p.m.).

Memphis King: 1902 Van Vranken Avenue, Schenectady, 372-5464. Call to pick up or just stop in and take out. They know how to do it here. Pulled pork, ribs, brisket to die for, and mouthwatering sides to go with. If you haven't stumbled across this place yet, make sure you do soon.

Mexican Radio: 325 State Street, Schenectady, 621-3700. Beautiful-looking place, right smack in the middle of downtown. What we had was OK generic Mexican. It is perfectly located, comfortable to eat in and, we think, a real plus for the downtown area. We went to a big private party there and service was terrific, and everyone was happy.

Moon and River Café: 115 Ferry Street, Schenectady, 382-1938. This little café in the middle of the Stockade District offers vegetarian and lighter fare, with an eclectic mix of music and performance during the open mics.

Peter Pause Restaurant: 535 Nott Street, Schenectady, 382-9278. This little place across from Union College changed hands after 40 years in 2014. They still haven't gotten their groove yet, but it's such a cool diner-esque experience, we'll hold out some hope for it. Early breakfast and lunch. Try their other place, **Newest Lunch** at 715 Albany Street, Schenectady, 377-6580, for a great old-time diner breakfast, lunch, or early dinner. Excellent soups, their famous hot dogs with meat sauce, and a full menu of other family pleasers.

Pinhead Susan's: 38–40 Broadway, Schenectady, 346-6431. This is one of those friendly Irish pubs, with great beer and music, and excellent pub food. A college favorite, it's still fun for the family, and a great place to go after a show downtown. Check out their website to read the story of how they got their name (www.pinheadsusan.com).

Pizza King: 124 Jay Street, Schenectady, 393-7440. Still one of our favorites for great pizzas with unusual toppings.

Scotti's Restaurant: 1730 Union Street, Schenectady, 393-7440. One of the best neighborhood Italian restaurants in the area. Open since 1966, Scotti's offers a friendly atmosphere, an affordable menu, and a pizza that tastes close to a real New York-style pizza.

Tara Kitchen: 431 Liberty Street, Schenectady, 708-3485. If you want to do something very nice for your taste buds today, stop in to Tara Kitchen for lunch or dinner to savor some excellent Moroccan food.

Delicious pairing of flavors you won't find anywhere else. Their sauces are so popular they are now sold at Price Chopper, Whole Foods, and Honest Weight Food Co-op (others listed on their web page). Since they opened in 2012, they have consistently been voted one of the top 10 restaurants in the Capital District.

Thai Thai Bistro: 268 State Street, Schenectady, 372-1111. When you just really need good Thai food. This funky, little place is near the theater, serves up all your favorite Thai dishes, and has a bar. Service is great with reasonable prices. Can't really go wrong here.

Union Café: 1725 Union Street, Schenectady, 280-1600. If you want Greek food done right, this is where to come. Every Greek dish is perfect, delicious, and served by a delightful staff. Come back for their deli sandwiches; their rueben is a killer. You can get breakfast all day, and if you're running late, call it in and pick it up. Nice patio for outside dining.

Pizza

There are pizza places all over town and we're sure you'll find one you like. Our short list in or near the downtown areas includes the following:

Big Apple Pizza: 108 14th Street, Troy, 271-4444. Located on the RPI campus. We love this pizza, and you can pick up a large cheese pizza that is actually large, but with a small price.

Fountain Restaurant: 283 New Scotland Avenue, Albany, 482-9898.

Jonathan's Pizza: 31 North Pearl Street, Albany, 463-5100.

I Love Pizza: 125 4th Street, Troy, 274-0071.

La Famiglia: 1770 Central Avenue, Colonie, 452-1234. Enormous, delicious pizza.

Paesan's Pizza & Restaurant: 289 Ontario Street, Albany, 435-0312.

Pizza King: 124 Jay Street, Schenectady, 347-1234.

SoHo Pizza: 269 Lark Street, Albany, 427-1111.

Sovrana Pizza and Deli: 63 North Lake Street, Albany, 465-0961. One of the best in Albany. Delicious homemade crust. Large pie for little $.

Worth a special trip:

DeFazio's Pizzeria: 266 4th Street in Troy's Little Italy, 271-1111. This is where you'll find wood-fired pizza with a crispy crust and tart sauce. The four-cheese pizza is sublime. Look for their new restaurant opening up the street.

Let's Shop!

First, here's an overview of some of the shopping areas. Pleasant places to stroll and shop include:

Lark Street in downtown Albany boasts small art and gift shops and little restaurants and coffee shops throughout.

Delaware Avenue in downtown Albany also has a number of great food places and some up-and-coming gift shops.

River Street in Troy is the location of antique shops, art galleries, gift shops, and clothing stores, with great places to eat mixed in.

Jay Street, Schenectady, is divided into the pedestrian shopping end (the 100s) and North Jay, where you will find Perreca's and Cornell's in Little Italy. Shopping on the pedestrian side is fun, with an eclectic assortment of funkier stores and eateries.

Upper Union, Schenectady, is where you will find useful service shops mixed in with some little stores and Gershon's Deli.

Newton Plaza, Route 9, Newtonville, is the home of an assortment of specialty stores and restaurants, including a Bruegger's Bagels. This section of Route 9 in Latham is becoming an endless stream of mini strips malls, but with some very nice stores and eateries in the mix.

Remsen Street in Cohoes has a number of small places you can shop, including a couple of antique stores, a bicycle shop and a bimonthly flea market. Businesses really come and go here, so you really don't know what you'll find when you get there. Pretty city with a great river view at the falls.

The Malls

Crossgates is the monster mall with its huge Regal Crossgates Stadium 18 and IMAX theaters and hundreds of shops. Crossgates Commons next door has a Walmart (the largest in the United States), Michaels, Sears Outlet, and an Ollie's Bargain Outlet, among other stores.

Colonie Center is also pretty big—now with a Whole Foods, as well as a giant L.L. Bean and Barnes & Noble. Some new restaurants and a Regal Cinema (with stadium seating) make this one a comfortable alternative to Crossgates.

The **Colonie Center shopping district** extends east to west along Central Avenue and north along Wolf Road, and it includes a Trader Joe's.

Central Avenue, west of Albany, is a nonstop collection of strip malls.

Northway Mall/Target Plaza is across Central Avenue from Colonie Center with a Target, Marshalls, Eddie Bauer, Jo-Ann Fabrics, and more, including a BJ's Wholesale Club and a Lowe's.

The Shoppes at Latham Circle currently include Lowe's, Bob's Discount Furniture Store, a Burlington Coat Factory and a supersized Walmart. A number of other smaller stores will eventually fill out the newly built shopping destination.

Stuyvesant Plaza is an open-air mall with smaller quality shops, and restaurants, including the wonderful Book House.

Latham Farms, on Route 7 in Latham, contains a Sam's Club, Home Depot, Dick's, and a Hannaford supermarket, along with a handful of other stores.

Clifton Park Center off Route 146 (exit 9 from the Northway I-87) 70 or so stores including Boscovs, JC Penney, Home Goods plus a Regal Cinema. Hop down the road to Route 9 to find **The Crossing** which is home to Target, Kohls, Office Max and Home Depot. If you still need to shop, head south along Route 9 where an endless array of mini-malls awaits you.

Not everywhere will have everything you want or need, so we're arranging shopping by categories. We will start with the most important things.

Chocolate

Aldi: 307 Columbia Turnpike, East Greenbush. Yes, we know this is a grocery store, but it's a German-owned discount store that imports a lot of delicious German products, including chocolate. You can get huge bars of it here for about $4 per pound. The fruit-and-nut bar they carry is great. It contains hazelnuts, rather than peanuts, with sweet raisins in a very good chocolate. If chocolate is your main food group, you might want to try some here and save a ton of money at the same time.

Candy Kraft Candies: 2575 Western Avenue, Altamont, 355-1860. Great little candy store filled with everything you miss from when you were a kid. Delicious chocolates, ribbon candy, nuts, and gifts. You name it, they packed it in here.

Chocolate Gecko: If you're wondering where the Chocolate Gecko went, it was bought by Uncle Sam's Candy and is available at both of their stores (see below). Chocolate Gecko uses only natural, organic ingredients and produces a very nice selection of beautiful-looking chocolates. The flavors are subtle, sophisticated, and quite delicious.

Emack & Bolio's: 366 Delaware Avenue, Albany, 512-5100. Yes, this is an ice cream place, *and* a chocolate shop. They offer a limited but surprisingly good selection. Their turtles have peanuts rather than the traditional pecans, but are still very tasty. The store covers all of the bases here, with excellent ice cream and chocolate, a case of delicious baked goods (cookies, pastries, brownies), and assorted beverages. It also has live music and is adorable to boot.

Krause's Homemade Candy: 1609 Central Avenue, Albany, 869-3950. This is an Albany mainstay. The store is bright and cheerful, and just the right place to find a delicious gift. We really like their milk-chocolate turtles and caramels, but we find the flavor of some of their creams to be too overwhelming. Prices are at the lower end of the spectrum, which means you can indulge in some excellent chocolate without having to give up food for a week, although living on nothing but chocolate has a certain appeal.

Uncle Sam's Candy: 2571 Albany Street, Schenectady, 372-2243; Newton Plaza, 594 New Loudon Road, Latham, 608-4949. We like Uncle Sam's a lot. Their stores carry a very large assortment of handmade chocolate (including sugar free). Their creams are not over-the-top flavored like some, but are really good, as are their caramels. Their assorted chocolate barks are especially delicious. Their world-famous almond buttercrunch is addictive. The best thing here is the enormous selection of chocolates molded into almost any shape you can imagine, from cats to dogs to electronics to tools to farm animals. It comes in milk, dark, and white chocolate. Uncle Sam's also has the best licorice in town. You can order online and get to look at all of the chocolate shapes, too. Spend $50 and they'll ship for free. Not hard to do.

Our Fabulous Chocolate Cake

9 tablespoons cocoa
1-pound box of Domino dark brown sugar—the whole box (it makes a
    difference—Domino is less runny than cheaper brands)
1¼ sticks butter
1½ teaspoons vanilla
3 large eggs
2¼ cups flour
2 teaspoons baking soda
½ teaspoon salt
1 cup regular sour cream—not lowfat
1 cup boiling water

Mix the cocoa in with the brown sugar on low speed with a mixer. Melt butter and add to this mixture. Add vanilla and eggs, and mix well. Blend flour, baking soda, and salt, and add alternately with the sour cream into chocolate mixture. Once everything is thoroughly mixed, slowly add 1 cup of boiling water (this gives the baking soda a boost because it is such a heavy cake). Pour into two 9-inch round cake pans that have been greased and floured. Bake at 350 degrees for 35 minutes or until the center springs back. Remove from pans after about 10 minutes and let cool thoroughly.

For a merely fabulous cake, use your favorite frosting; ours is Betty Crocker's Classic Chocolate. For a stupendous cake, cut each layer into two even 9-inch circles. Beat 1 pint of heavy whipping cream until very stiff and add a few tablespoons of sugar to taste. Use 1/3 of the whipped cream between each layer. Encase in frosting (this will require two full cans). Refrigerate to set, then die happy.

Ice Cream

Bumpy's Polar Freeze: 2013 State Street, Schenectady, 395-3314. Full array of fast food: fish fry, hamburgers, finger food, etc., and 135(!) flavors of soft-serve ice cream. The plus here is the bumper boats and climbing walls.

Cold Stone Creamery: Stuyvesant Plaza, 1475 Western Avenue, Albany, 514-2003. Cold Stone specializes in an ice cream that is midway between hard-packed and soft-serve. Candy, nuts, and some flavorings are mixed in on a cold granite stone while you wait. A little pricey, but very good quality. It is open all year.

Emack & Bolio's: 366 Delaware Avenue, Albany, 512-5100. This great place for ice cream opened in summer 2008, serving not only really creamy, delicious ice cream in 20 flavors (not all vegetarian; be sure to ask first), but wonderful brownies, cookies, and a selection of chocolates. Great location on Delaware, near the Spectrum 8 Theatres.

Guptill's Coney Express: 1085 New Loudon Road (Route 9), Cohoes, 785-0660. The best thing about this place is that it usually opens weeks before anybody else, so when you are desperately craving that first ice cream cone of the season, this is the place to go. Their soft-serve is great and comes in flavors we love, and the hard-packed ice cream comes in a multitude of flavors as well. All delicious. Guptill's is located next to the roller rink, if you need some fun exercise to work off those delicious calories.

Jim's Tastee Freez: 58 Delaware Avenue, Delmar, 439-3912. A summertime staple. A Delmartian favorite. Good ice cream, fast food, and close to town.

Kurver Kreme: 1349 Central Avenue, Albany, 459-4120. This has been a local favorite forever. The soft-serve is good, although on a hot day it will melt before you reach your car. The pluses here are the variety of flavors and range of sizes and prices. They have a kids' cone that is just the right size, and cheap! Kurver Kreme's return after the long winter is one of the opening days we look forward to.

Lickety Split: 589 Columbia Turnpike, East Greenbush, 477-9517. The soft-serve here is a little waxy for our taste, but the variety of flavors and the hometown feel make this a popular tradition for local families. The Funplex is attached, making it a summertime destination.

Moxie's Ice Cream: 1344 Spring Avenue, Wynantskill, 283-4901. This place is really not that far out of Troy. Travel down Pawling Avenue and make a left on Spring Avenue. Moxie's is just a few miles down the road on the left, and definitely worth the trip. This is a family-run business that has been around for more than 40 years. Yes, there really is a Moxie, and yes, he knows how to make delicious ice cream. His daughter, Miss Pam, has been running the stand for the last number of years. The ice cream is rich (15 percent milkfat) and the flavors are numerous. By the time National Ice Cream Day arrives (third Sunday in July), Moxie's has almost 70 different flavors, including five different vanillas made from different beans from around the world. Moxie's is famous for its Blue Moon ice cream, an odd blue concoction of who-knows-what. In addition to great ice cream, the surrounding playground, with the best swings in the world, makes this place a treat in every way. Moxie's opens on Mother's Day. They close for the season when the ice cream runs out, usually in late August.

On the Farm: 273 Troy-Schenectady Road, Latham, 785-9930. This has been a Latham summertime fixture since 1986. They serve great soft-serve in the basic varieties, with one special thrown in every couple of weeks. On the Farm serves Edy's hard-packed ice cream if you're not into the soft-serve. They also have a lunch and dinner take-out menu (hamburgers, fish fry, french fries, etc.) that is pretty good. There are plenty of picnic tables and parking. We are always sad when their season ends in October. They sell Christmas trees here in late November.

The Snowman: 531 Fifth Avenue, Troy, 233-1714. This is one of our favorites, mostly because of the weird snowman logo, but the tasty ice cream is homemade and includes their own version of Blue Moon. Their black raspberry is sooooo good. Standing on line when they first open at the end of winter is one of our rites of spring. The soft-serve is smooth and thick. Although the parking lot doesn't offer the best ambience, you can walk down to the river near Melville's house and enjoy your ice cream there.

Stewart's Shops: All over. Yes, we're including Stewart's because their ice cream is actually good, available all year long, inexpensive, and everywhere. They have ice cream cone specials throughout the year, including St. Patrick's Day (you must wear green), and Mother's and Father's Day. They have a zillion flavors, which are all worth a try.

Toll Gate Ice Cream: 1569 New Scotland Road, Slingerlands, 439-9824. Family-run since 1949, Toll Gate sells delicious homemade ice cream. They probably have not updated their "décor" since the '50s, but that shouldn't stop you from trying out their wonderful flavors. They serve food, too.

Bakeries

Bake for You: 540 Delaware Avenue, Albany, 207-3430. A little place with a nice selection of baked goodies. They have scones. And tea. That's all we need. Get there early in the day if you want a good selection, because they bake what they bake and when it's gone, it's gone.

Bella Napoli: 672 New Loudon Road, Latham, 783-0196; 721 River Street, Troy, 274-8277. This is your full-service bakery, selling breads, pastries, rolls (their dinner butter rolls are amazing), donuts, specialty cookies, and cakes. The Latham store has a place to eat it all with some coffee. The mini elephant ears, almond horn cookies, and jelly donuts are especially delicious. Really, everything is.

Bountiful Bread: 1475 Western Avenue, Stuyvesant Plaza, 438-3540. They feature a variety of great European-style breads with crispy crusts, and wonderful, original sandwiches. Their soups are outstanding.

Bruegger's Bagels: 29 North Pearl Street, Albany; 55 Congress Street, Troy; and many other locations. Yes, this is a chain, but a chain that started in 1983, in Troy. And a chain that knows how to make some of the best bagels you'll ever have. The first Bruegger's is still located on Congress Street in Troy.

Cheesecake Machismo: 293 Hamilton Street, Albany, 427-7019. Buy a slice of homemade, delicious cheesecake, or buy the whole thing and die happy. Changing specials mean you can come over and over again to find your new favorite.

Cider Belly Doughnuts: 25 North Pearl Street, Albany, 253-4640. Oh sweet mama. Fresh, warm cider doughnuts in a variety of flavors, right in downtown. Even vegan ones. Sooooo delicious! We are so lucky.

Coccadotts Cake Shop: 1179 Central Avenue, Albany, 438-4937. Their specialty cakes are gorgeous and delicious, too. If you have your heart set on something memorable for your special day, they can make it.

Cookie Factory: 520 Congress Street, Troy, 268-1060. The Cookie Factory sells a familiar selection of Italian cookies and pastries from their really cool old building. You can find the Fudge Fantasy here, our favorite cookie. The staff is friendly and helpful.

Crisan Bakery & Edible Art Gallery: 197 Lark Street, Albany, 445-2727. Although they closed their café at the end of 2014 (much to our dismay), they still can make you the wedding cake of your dreams, and do still supply wholesale goods around town. Their pastries are really some of the best. Luckily, you can still savor their baking at the snack counter at the Spectrum Theatres.

Grandma's Country Pies and Restaurant: 1273 Central Avenue, Albany, 459-4585. Pies!

Joan's Cake Chateau: 285 Old Niskayuna Road, Latham, 783-6422. This little house of a cake shop has been turning out lovely special-occasion cakes since 1980. Original designs and delicious, too. Let her bake you something special.

Make Me a Cake Next Door: 378 Delaware Avenue, Delmar, 439-4040. Beautiful cakes and cupcakes. Delicious, too. A friend brought us a box of their cupcakes, which we devoured without an ounce of guilt.

Perreca's Bakery: 33 North Jay Street, Schenectady, 372-1875. Perreca's has the best Italian bread in the area. Actually, anywhere.

Panera Bread: Everywhere, check the phone book. Good, in-house baked goods, but great soups and sandwiches to eat in or take out. Buy a whole brownie pie (not just a slice) and you'll be in heaven sooner.

The Placid Baker: 250 Broadway, Troy, 326-2657. We were so happy when they made Troy their home. They had been traveling to the Troy farmer's market only on weekends, so we'd have to wait to get our bread then. But now great, fresh breads all the time, tasty sandwiches, and delicious treats to go with. The hermit cookies are a favorite, but the mudslide cookies are also hard to resist.

Psychedelicatessen: 275 River Street, Troy, 478-3459. Amazing bagels you can get by the bagful, or have something delicious put on them. You can't even see the bagel through the poppy seeds on the ones we got. Amazing!! Did we say that already? We got some to go, and had to turn around and get a dozen more. We were told they freeze great, so we tried it and they do.

Schuyler Bakery: 637 Third Avenue, Watervliet, 273-0142. This is a great little bakery with a large selection of very inexpensive baked goods. The crumb buns are a personal favorite. They make a really good Easter bread, which we look forward to all year.

The Troy Waterfront Farmer's Market: The farmer's market hosts several bread, cookie, and pastry bakers including Dutch Desserts (Kinderhook), Mrs. London's (Saratoga), Our Daily Bread (Chatham), Placid Baker (Troy), Sweet Sue's (Troy), and Country Hearth (Valatie; gluten-free).

Villa Italia: 226 Broadway, Schenectady, 355-1144. The fancy Italian pastries (more than 40 mini varieties) here are beautiful to look at but better to eat. If you are in need of a wedding cake, they can make you one that's a work of art.

Zachary's Pastry Shoppe: 390 Columbia Turnpike, East Greenbush, 477-2140. The pastries here are almost too pretty to eat, but don't let that stop you—you won't be disappointed. They have a full selection of familiar and tasty standards and a lot of unusual and delectable others.

Wine and Spirits

Albany Distilling Company: 78 Montgomery Street (next to the Pump Station), Albany, 621-7191. Small operation, great whiskeys, now rum and vodka, too. Product available on site or all over the Capital District. Check their website: www.albanydistilling.com.

All Star Wine & Spirits: 579 Troy-Schenectady Road (Latham Farms), Latham, 220-9463. This is a wine superstore with such an enormous selection from all over the world, you can browse forever. All price ranges are available. The employees know their wines and are very helpful with good suggestions.

Empire Wine and Liquor: 1440 Central Avenue (Northway Mall), Colonie, 694-8503. We like this place. It has great prices on the standards and a good wine selection. We have tried some of the $5 imports, which were surprisingly good. Always busy, but fast checkout.

Nine Pin Ciderworks: 929 Broadway, Albany, 449-9999. Their signature hard ciders are available in store and around town, and there's a rotating array of experimental ones for tasting.

Oliver's Beverage Center: 105 Colvin Avenue, Albany, 459-2767, and its sister store, **Westmere Beverage:** 1756 Western Avenue, Albany, 456-1100. Together, the Brew Crew, 1,600 kinds of beer. Voted the best beer store forever because it is. You cannot be disappointed here.

Smith's Colonie Liquor Store: 1701 Central Avenue, Albany, 869-6671. Don't just give this one a drive-by thinking it's just another liquor store—stop in for a surprisingly large wine selection with OK prices. Getting in and out is tough on Central Avenue, so plan your timing to avoid rush hour.

The Wine Shop: 265 New Scotland Avenue, Albany, 438-1116. This is one of the great little places in Albany. There's no need to have your own wine cellar when you can find an extraordinary selection of wines from all over and in all price ranges right here. The staff is knowledgeable and helpful.

Yankee Distillers: 5 Fairchild Square, Clifton Park, 406-3245. Another craft alcohol establishment. Their aged rye and bourbon whiskies are both excellent. You can stop in for a tasting.

Farmer's Markets: all over, and they all have one or more of the local vineyards represented. We've seen Nine Pin, Brown's, and other local nectars wherever we go.

Delis and Specialty Markets

Andy's Italian Food & Deli: 256 Delaware Avenue, 463-2754. Walk into Andy's and you will want to eat everything in there. You can order big delicious sandwiches and Italian specialties to go; you will never have to cook again. The soups from Andy's grandma's recipes are so good and so filling; a small container and a piece of bread makes a complete meal.

Asian Supermarket: 1245 Central Avenue, Albany, 438-8886. This is the big place to shop for Asian food specialties, including groceries, meat, seafood, and dry goods. A real supermarket with lots of selection.

Asian Food Market: 91 Colvin Avenue, Albany, 458-8166. Smaller grocery with a very good selection of Asian specialties. Some things you won't find at the bigger stores. Worth checking out.

Cardona's Market: 340 Delaware Avenue, Albany, 434-4838. This is another great Italian deli/grocery that is just a short walk from the Spectrum. This market has everything; the store is bigger than you think, and everything is fresh and delicious. They have great prepared foods, salads, more olives than you can imagine, cookies, and extremely good help.

Delmar Marketplace and McCarroll's The Village Butcher: 406 Kenwood Avenue, Delmar; Marketplace 439-3936; McCarroll's 478-9651. Quality fresh meats and deli are what you'll find here. There is an excellent selection of prepared meals to heat at home, as well as a good organic and local food selection. Microbrews!

Euro Deli and Market: 231 Wade Road Ext., Latham, 785-0103. This place is an unexpected find tucked into the far end of the Target strip mall in Latham. It is a true Polish market with amazing meats, cheeses, and frozen pierogis of every kind. Fabulous mustards, sauerkrauts, pickles, you name it. Everything to create a Polish feast.

Genoa Importing: 435 Loudon Road, Loudonville, 427-0078. Quality imported foods can be found here, in addition to gourmet meals to take out, and fresh bread. Sandwiches, soups, and delicious subs to go.

Halal Market: 264 Central Avenue, Albany, 426-4194. The market specializes in halal meat. Big, well-stocked, and helpful. There are several similar specialty stores in this area of Central Avenue.

Honest Weight Food Co-op: 100 Watervliet Avenue, Albany, 482-2667. This is a member-owned co-op and one of the great things you'll find in Albany. Fresh natural produce, fish and meats, cheeses, bulk items, and basically everything you need to eat well and happily. If you haven't been, you should go. Lots more parking at this location.

India Bazaar: 1321 Central Avenue, Albany, 459-3108. This is a large Indian specialty market, everything you'll need to prepare delicious meals, so many spices, and they have Indian movies, too.

Kim's Asian Market: 1649 Central Avenue, Colonie, 452-2620. Kim's is a mostly Korean market, with Chinese and Japanese specialty foods. Fresh Asian produce, flours, etc.

Nora's Grocery: 143 Troy-Schenectady Road (in the Hilltop Plaza), Watervliet, 274-9393. This is another place you'd never find, but the Hilltop Plaza has had a number of really cool businesses come and go. Nora's is a small place chock-full with an outstanding selection of Middle Eastern ingredients and spices. Spices you won't find anywhere else. All kinds of feta cheese and delicious homemade dishes to go, including their fabulous stuffed grape leaves. Falafel, too. Well worth a visit.

Ragonese Italian Imports: 409 New Scotland Avenue, Albany, 482-2358. Mediterranean gourmet foods can be bought here.

Rolf's Pork Store: 70 Lexington Avenue, Albany, 463-0185. This has been an Albany meat store for more than 150 years, and a German-family-run one for four generations (Rolf's opened in 1968). The specialty meats are fresh and delicious. The German potato salad is the best anywhere, and they carry a ton of German imports, including crossword puzzles, cookies, candy, and the best cough drops made with real fruit juice. Stop in—they are really friendly.

Roma Foods Importing Co.: 9 Cobbee Road, Latham, 785-7480. Roma offers Italian food galore with some good salads. Fresh mozzarella, some nice imports, especially the sweets. They also have a pretty complete selection of the Twining loose teas in cans. Walk through the arch to get to the meat store featuring fresh, organic food.

Uncle Sam's Natural Foods: 77 4th Street, Troy, 271-7299; 646 New Loudon Road, Latham, 782-5233. This is a great natural-food store right in downtown Troy (and Latham, too) with a large selection of organic foods and products, including organic milk in glass bottles. The Troy store's sign with Uncle Sam is a hoot.

Apple Orchards

Altamont Orchards: 6654 Dunnsville Road, Altamont, 861-6515. The orchard features apples, a large farm stand, bedding plants, and donuts!

Bowman Orchards: 141 Sugar Hill Road, Rexford, 371-2042. Bowman grows dozens of varieties of apples, including our favorites: galas and empires. Berry picking begins in June. Donuts and cider are available, too.

Devoe's Rainbow Orchard: 1569 Halfmoon Parkway (Route 9), Clifton Park. 371-8397. U-don't pick here, but they do, from their 100-year-old orchard. They have a year-round store filled with goodies along with their delicious apples.

Goold Orchards: 1297 Brookview Station Road, Castleton, 732-7317. Apple Fest is always Columbus Day weekend, and features music, crafts, local wine, and of course, apples.

Indian Ladder Farms: 342 Altamont Road, Altamont, 765-2956. It's located at the base of the Helderbergs, and you can enjoy the view as you pick apples or berries, or while shopping for fresh veggies. You can even get up close and personal to some real farm animals.

Lindsey's Idyllwood Orchard: 267 Sugar Hill Road, Rexford, 371-5785. Seasonal apple picking at the orchard, but their store at 1537 Route 9 in Clifton Park is open year round, with local produce, baked goods, gifts, cider and, well, apples.

Riverview Orchards: 600 Riverview Road, Rexford, 371-2174. Although the apple picking is seasonal, the country store is open year-round with local food, crafts, and of course delicious apple cider donuts!

Our Own Apple Pie

We are not pie-crust snobs, so get yourself some Pillsbury ready-made and begin, or you can use your grandma's recipe, whichever you like.

Crust *(bottom only)*
Use a 9-inch pan so you'll have more pie, and press the Pillbury or roll out your own and get set to start building your pie.

Apples
We like to use at least three varieties: one for sweetness like Macs, one for a little tartness like Granny Smiths, and one fleshier to absorb some

of the soup, like Delicious. There are many varieties of each kind, so pick your favorite in each category.

You will need:
8–10 apples, peeled, cored, and thinly sliced
$1/2$ cup sugar
$1/3$ cup flour
$1^1/2$ teas. cinnamon

Mix the dry ingredients together and start layering your pie. One layer of apples. Sprinkle with sugar mixture. Next layer of apples. Sprinkle with sugar mixture. Keep doing this until you have a nice high mound of apples and sugar, or run out of apples (about $4^1/2$ inches high in the middle). Place pie on a lined cookie sheet before you proceed.

If you still have any sugar left, you can throw it in with this:

$1/2$ cup dark brown sugar
$1/3$ cup flour
$1/3$ cup white sugar
$1/2$ cup of margarine sliced into all of the above

You need to get your hands dirty here, so wash them first. Then stick them in the bowl with all the ingredients and blend them thoroughly until you get a crumbly mixture. Add a little more flour if it is not crumbly enough—not too much though. Evenly coat the top of your apples with the crumb mixture. Use all of it, and then lick your hands off—they will be delicious. Then wash them.

So the crust doesn't burn, attach 3 to 4 pieces of 3-inch aluminum foil strips and cover the pie-crust edge with it before baking. You can also tent the pie with another piece of foil for the first 25 minutes.

Bake at 350 degrees for an hour plus maybe 10 minutes. Check doneness by spearing the apples to see if they are soft. When they are, take the pie out and let it cool and settle.

Enjoy!

Stuff

Books

Barnes & Noble is locally represented in the malls. It's still nice to have a big bookstore to browse through and find something good to read.

The Book House: Stuyvesant Plaza, 1475 Western Avenue, Albany, 489-4761. These are the same people who own Market Block Books in Troy. They love books and it shows. The Little Book House is ideal for children as well, with some really sweet children's books.

Dove & Hudson: 296 Hudson Avenue (at the corner of Dove and Hudson), 432-4518. This is the best used bookstore in all the land. The quality and range shows that the books here have been carefully selected and not just collected to take up shelf space. We want to read everything in here. Go. Go now!

I Love Books: 380 Delaware Avenue, Delmar, 478-0715. This shop offers a moderate selection of new books, but has a large selection of great cards and gifts.

Lyrical Ballad Bookstore: 7 Phila Street, Saratoga, 584-8779. Nonfiction, art, and antiquarian books can be found in a labyrinth of an old bank. If you can't find that rare book you've been looking for, it just might be here.

Market Block Books: 290 River Street, Troy, 328-0045. This store is a nice addition to Troy's downtown, offering a good selection, lots of local lore, and a great browsing atmosphere.

Mary Jane Books: 215 Western Avenue, Albany, 465-2238. You don't browse here, you just bring your textbook list and they will get it for you. They buy and sell thousands of college texts efficiently and painlessly.

M.O.S.S. Books: 51 Congress Street, Troy, 274-0199. The Russell Sage bookstore attached to Bruegger's Bagels has textbooks upstairs and a current-release bookstore and gift shop downstairs.

Open Door Bookstore: 128 Jay Street, Schenectady, 346-2719. This is a really nice bookstore, where you feel right at home right away and can find books you want just inside the doors. They also carry a good selection of fun gifts.

Whitney Book Corner: 600 Union Street, Schenectady (Schenectady Public Library) and **William K. Sanford Library:** 629 Albany Shaker Road, Albany. Both of these libraries sell used, read once, donated books, and library discards at unbelievable prices. We never come away with less than 20. Check back on a regular basis as donations seem to run with the seasons.

Comic Book Stores

Aquilonia: 412 Fulton Street, Troy, 271-1069. This is the best comic book store on earth, near Troy.

Earthworld: 537 Central Avenue, Albany, 459-2400. The other best comic book store on earth, near Albany.

Excellent Adventures Comics: 110 Milton Avenue, Ballston Spa, 884-9498. We know this is a little out of town, but these guys have a ton of great old comic books at really good prices.

Zombie Planet: 1238 Central Avenue, Albany, 438-7202. Comics and graphic novels, but their specialty is role-playing games. They have tons of them as well as collectibles, action figures and more!

Hardware Stores

A. Philips Hardware Inc.: Seven area locations, including 1157 Central Avenue, Albany, 459-2300; 1729 Union Street, Schenectady, 346-4383; 235 Delaware Avenue, Delmar, 439-9943. Phillips Hardware is a small chain based in Albany, around for more than 125 years, whose focus is on service. It is a real hardware store with all of the stuff you need to fix all of the broken stuff you have. They also make keys.

DeLollo's: 701 19th Street, Watervliet, 274-7019. The friendliest hardware store you'll find. The store has almost everything, and if they don't, they can probably get it for you.

Harbor Freight Tools: 1770 Central Avenue, Suite 4, Albany, 452-3875. OK, so who hasn't been lured in by one of their ads? The prices are unbelievable, and they have those odd little tools made for one specific job that you don't want to spend a fortune on, and only has to last for the one job you're buying it for. This place is one of our entertainment venues, just to see what they have and for how cheap. Bonus—They are right next door to La Famiglia Pizzeria, 452-1234, which has one of the best pizzas in the area. No kidding.

Pfeil Hardware & Paint: 63 Third Street, Troy, 687-0014. If a bright, beautiful hardware store makes you swoon, stop in and visit this two-floor, chock-full delight.

Shaker Ace Hardware: 607 Watervliet Shaker Road, Latham, 785-9052. Another one of our favorites. What you need is somewhere in this store, and one of Shaker's helpful hardware people will find it for you.

Computer Supplies and Parts

ABI Computers: 90 Hoosick Street, Troy, 270-9933. This is a small retail and repair shop with new, new-in-box older, and used components and a knowledgeable and friendly owner.

A&G Computers: 614 19th Street, Watervliet, 274-5123. This is a small, family-owned shop with retail parts and repair for almost any system. They also make house calls.

Computer Renaissance: 595 New Loudon Road, Latham, 220-4445. This is a retail and repair shop with an emphasis on customer service and newer systems and supplies. They sell a lot of refurbished systems that can fit any budget (www.comprenny.com).

eLot Electronics Recycling: 64 Hannay Lane, Glenmont, 266-9385. "Recycle. Reuse. Recover." Don't discard your old mercury light bulbs, batteries, and electronics in a landfill—they generate toxic waste, and eLot recovers and reuses as much as possible. The store has a large used component selection, so you can build your own.

Electronics Parts and Supplies

Grimmer's Electronic Supply: 41 North Brandywine Avenue, Schenectady, 374-8480. Grimmer's is an old-fashioned electronics supply store with a tube tester. Very helpful.

Trojan Electronic Supply: 15 Middleburg Street, Troy, 274-4481. The store looks like an old barn on the outside and it is one on the inside, but electronics nerds swoon when they enter this parts-and-components retail store/museum. Do you need a No. 49 2V flashlight bulb? Try finding it on the web. Trojan Electronic Supply has it. Do you need a brand new LCD oscilloscope? They've got that, too.

Bicycle Shops

CK Cycles (formerly Klarsfeld Cyclery): 1370 Central Avenue, Albany, 459-3272. This shop has been around forever. They know bikes and have a high-quality selection of bikes and accessories. Excellent repair service.

Downtube Bicycle Works: 466 Madison Avenue, Albany (across from Washington Park), 434-1711. Great bikes for the whole family, and really friendly service. You can get it fixed here, too.

Freemans Bridge Sports, Inc.: 38 Freemans Bridge Road, Scotia, 382-0593 (just over the bridge from Schenectady). This is a serious bike shop for the serious rider, with a great selection of bicycles and accessories. But also great for us—we got our unicycle, and a terrific folding bike here. Expert repairs, too.

Plaine and Son: 1816 State Street, Schenectady, 346-1433. Plaine and Son boasts a *large*, full-service shop. This is their flagship store; they have a couple of newer ones around with different names, which all offer a good selection of bikes and expert service.

Sycaway Bicycle Sales and Service: 13 Lord Avenue (off Hoosick Street), Troy, 273-7788. This is a really friendly shop with a selection of better bicycles. As the name says: service for your broken bicycles as well.

Repair and Recycle Bikes

Troy Bike Rescue: This is a volunteer-run bicycle resource center where you can get help fixing your bike or get connected with one that needs adopting. In Troy, 3280 6th Avenue, 328-4827; Albany, 15 Trinity Place basement (near Madison). Contact www.troybikerescue.org.

Clothing

Aurora's Boutique: 286 River Street, Troy, 266-1191. Upscale women's clothing (mostly formal wear). This boutique features styles by Ursula of Switzerland, lovely jewelry, accessories, and some really nice vintage accents.

B. Lodge & Co.: 75 North Pearl Street, Albany, 463-4646. Albany's oldest store. You have to go, just because. Carries the basics—underwear, socks, t-shirts, and work clothing. You can find items you didn't know they still made, along with everything else. Feels like stepping back in time.

Enigma.co: 16 1st Street, Troy, 308-8422. US-made designer clothing for men. That's right. A really cool store for men's clothing, right in downtown Troy.

Fancy Schmancy: 641 New Loudon Road, Latham, 452-1269. Looking for that perfect dress for the next big event? Fancy Schmancy carries a large selection of beautiful formalwear, designer shoes and bags, gorgeous costume jewelry and accessories, and hats that would make Mary Lou Whitney jealous.

Lollipops Children's Shop: 594 New Loudon Road, Latham, 786-0379. The kids' clothes here are so cute you'll want them in your size. This is where you drag grandma to buy something special for her precious grandchildren.

The Shoppe: 260 Broadway, Troy, 273-0202. Expanding from its flagship store in downtown Saratoga, the Shoppe brings its designer duds to Troy in this lovely shop. Beautiful dresses for all occasions, accessories, Frye boots, and much more.

Sweater Venture: 700 Columbia Turnpike, East Greenbush, 477-9317. Not just sweaters—although they have an amazing selection of hand-knit sweaters from around the world—but also jewelry, gifts, the funkiest of hats, gloves, scarves, and the nicest store cat in the area. This store is well worth the short trip. They have special sales throughout the year during which you can get some great deals.

Truly Rhe: 1 Broadway, Troy, 414-3876. This is a beautiful shop with lovely women's clothing and accessories, ranging from casual to elegant. Some unique pieces, as well as a gently used rack.

Furniture Stores

Huck Finn's Warehouse: 25 Erie Boulevard, Albany, 465-3373. This is a big place with lots of merchandise to choose from and the best carpet selection around.

Kincaid Home Furnishings: 801 New Loudon Road, Latham, 783-1850. Kincaid features high-end, absolutely gorgeous furniture that will hold up for generations.

Kugler's Red Barn: 425 Consaul Road, Colonie, 370-2468. This is a furniture store that's actually in a red barn and sells solid country and Shaker styles made by small quality companies right here in the United States.

Mooradians Furniture: 800 Central Avenue, Albany, 489-2529. In business for 75 years, this store carries a full line of furniture for the whole house at good prices, and they offer quick delivery, too.

Old Brick Furniture: 2910 Campbell Road, Schenectady, 377-1600; 33–37 Warehouse Row (on Railroad Avenue), Albany, 438-9600; 2 River Street, Troy, 273-2000. Old Brick sells solid, beautiful furniture—the kind you can pass down to the next generation—at great prices.

Taft Furniture: 1960 Central Avenue, Albany, 456-3361. This is a huge furniture store/warehouse—hey, it is "the big store"—with everything you need for your home.

Antique, Thrift, and Retro Sources

The Antiques Warehouse: 78 4th Street, Troy, 441-3950. This is an enormous warehouse of antique furniture and accessories. Always getting in "new" pieces. Some very cool. A big plus is the upholstery service they have. It's hard to find a good upholsterer, but we had a couple of things done and they look fabulous.

The Closet Shop: 337 Delaware Avenue, Delmar, 439-5722. Upscale, gently used clothing and accessories. Designer names, thrifty prices.

Community Closet Thrift Shop: 146 Remsen Street, Cohoes. Here you'll find clothing and household items all at a price *you* set.

Coxsackie Antique Center: 12400 State Route 9W, West Coxsackie, 731-8888. The antique center features items from more than 100 dealers. Shopping here is more fun than you can imagine, and they have everything.

Fifi's Frocks and Frills: 1811 Western Avenue, Albany (Westmere Shopping Center), 869-1677. Terrific consignment shop to get your designer clothes and accessories at really good prices. Bright, cheerful, fun place to shop.

For Pete's Sake "A Thrifty Place": 583 New Scotland Avenue, Albany (corner of South Allen and New Scotland), 525-1107. Connected with St. Peter's Hospital, this shop offers nice, usually upscale clothing at unbelievable prices. Something for everyone.

Funcycled: 272 River Street, Troy, 629-5386. "Furniture repurposing." Taking pieces whose time has gone and making them something fun and useable again. Bright, cheery place.

Goodwill: 720 Hoosick Street, Troy, 272-8451. This is the Goodwill superstore, carrying lots of new, discontinued, and used clothing.

Goodwill: 1 Fuller Road, Albany, 459-5580. Goodwill stores don't seem to have quite the eclectic selection that Salvation Army has, but offer weekly specials for everyone. Goodwill is open on Sunday, and all of the half-price items from the previous week are discounted even further.

Great Finds Thrift Boutique: 260 Washington Avenue, Albany, 449-7715. Hats and gently used clothing for women can be purchased here at low prices. The shop is open weekdays and late for First Fridays.

Liz's Closet: 1762 Western Avenue, Albany, 452-1001. Liz's has been around for 25 years. This is a consignment shop with better-quality clothes at good prices.

Metropolis Vintage: 32 Fuller Road, Albany, 438-8277. This is where you get the vintage dress of your dreams and the fabulous jewelry to go with it. The cooler kind of antiques as well.

Niskayuna Antiques (used to be White House Flea Market): 3901 State Street, Schenectady, 346-7851. A very long time ago, this shop was located in an actual white house in downtown Schenectady; however, it has moved a few times, and is now in the old Duane's Toyland store. Antiques and collectibles from 40 vendors are all inside; good hours.

One Kind Mobile Boutique: Eco-friendly, recycled, upcycled, mostly clothing store, with some nice handmade items added in. As the name implies, this Troy-based shop moves around. Check their Facebook page to find them.

Patricia's Room: 162 Jay Street, Schenectady, 396-7512. Great selection of retro pieces and the funkier kind of antiques.

Plato's Closet: 818 Central Avenue, Albany, 459-3104; 2330 Watt Street (Crosstown Plaza), Schenectady, 688-0514. This is the place to buy and sell gently used teen/junior clothing.

Ravena Barn Flea Market and Thrift Shop: Route 9W, Ravena (1/3 mile south of the Ravena traffic light), 756-7778. A whole lot of everything.

Salvation Army: 452 Clinton Avenue, Albany, 465-2416; Troy-Schenectady Road, Latham, 783-7120. The Latham location has a pretty interesting selection of merchandise and discounts. Furniture has a fast turnover, with the occasional very cool retro piece, so stop back frequently. The new store in Latham on Route 2 is huge.

Silver Fox Salvage: 20 Learned Street, Albany (behind the old Miss Albany Diner, now Tanpopo), 265-1836. Love this place. You never know what kind of cool piece you will find. Last time we came home with an antique "ice box" which only needed a new paint job. Cement garden statuary outside, bits and pieces of all sorts everywhere. Check with them to have something custom built for you.

Something Olde, Something New: 1969 New Scotland Road, Slingerlands, 475-0663. This shop offers better secondhand women's clothing and a good selection of furniture. There are a lot of very cool retro housewares as well. Good prices.

Treasure Chest Thrift Store: 295 Hamilton Street, Albany, 436-7451. Proceeds from purchases you make here go to the Damien Center, which helps those living with AIDS and HIV. The shop offers a nice selection of clothing and housewares.

Treasure Cove Thrift Shop: 135 Adams Street, Delmar, 439-9976. Clothing, shoes, knick-knacks, jewelry. Church thrift shop, so hours are limited.

The Trojan Horse: Frear Building, 2 3rd Street, Troy, 376-2670. Although a number of the antique stores left Troy, the Trojan Horse has moved to bigger digs with great lighting, and has even more good stuff than before. Nice paintings, too. There are some beautiful pieces here.

Twilight Vintage Clothing: 44 4th Street, Troy, 326-2211. Go upstairs to this vintage clothing store to find some pretty cool stuff.

For the Dogs (and Cats and Other Creatures, Too)

Benson's Pet Center: 197 Wolf Road, Albany, 435-1738 (more locations around the Capital District; check online). Benson's supplies everything your pet needs, including food, toys, and medications.

Davey Jones Locker: 386 Delaware Avenue, Albany, 436-4810. Everything your scalier variety of pet could need is here.

Eddie's Aquarium Centre: 1254 New Loudon Road, Latham, 783-3474 (783-FISH). The staff at Eddie's are expert in the fish and reptile worlds. The store has everything you could possibly need.

Healthy Pet Center: 237 North Greenbush Road, Troy, 283-4027; 154 Delaware Avenue, Delmar, 487-4587; 775 New Loudon Road, Latham, 785-7387. These family-owned stores feature a great selection, friendly service, grooming, and training.

Henry Loves Betty: 195 River Street, Troy, 744-8277. The most adorable pet store ever. All-natural and organic treats for your beloved, plus collars, toys, clothing, and much more. They have an Uncle Sam pull toy! How perfect is that?

PetSmart: Latham Farms, 609 Troy-Schenectady Road, Latham, 785-4621. This is your full-service pet superstore, and they have everything, including adoption clinics from local shelters.

Pet Supplies Plus: 1235 Western Avenue, Albany, 438-1040. One of the places for great selection and prices. Fun just to walk the aisles.

Creative Supplies

A.C. Moore: 873 New Loudon Road, Latham, 782-0095. If you just don't know what to do with your spare time, you can certainly find some little project to work on in here. They don't really specialize in one specific craft area, but you can probably find something close to what you need.

Albany Art Room: 350 New Scotland Avenue, Albany, 915-1091. Art supplies, art gifts, and books are available in the store, but the Albany Art Room also offers art classes and/or work space for artists at all levels.

Arlene's Artist Materials: 57 Fuller Road, Albany, 482-8881. Yes, this is a great art supply store, and fun to just walk around in to see what you didn't know you needed; however, it also has a great selection of postcards and greeting cards, which are a lot less boring than the grocery-store variety. Large selection of ready-to-use frames, but will custom frame anything.

Jo-Ann Fabrics and Crafts: 1440 Central Avenue (in the Northway Mall), Albany, 459-5026. One of the last all-purpose fabric stores in the area, JoAnn's carries lots of fleece, dress-up fabrics, and quilting supplies. The home-décor fabrics are pretty good, too—they can special order for you as well. The craft department is limited but OK. Online shopping with them is sometimes easier during the big sales, and you can still use the same coupons.

Hill's Stationery: 451 Broadway, Troy, 274-1080. Office, art, and drafting supplies can be found on the shelves here. All your printing needs, too.

Joyful Quilter: 19 Glenridge Road, Glenville, 399-0128. Quality quilting fabrics, books, notions, special events. Check their calendar.

Michaels: 579 Troy-Schenectady Road (Latham Farms), Latham, 783-4358. Another all-in-one craft, art, flower, and framing place. Nice bead and yarn selection, limited art supplies, plenty of frames, and tons of scrapbooking, paper, and card stuff.

Northeast Ceramic Supply: 10 Monroe Street, Troy, 274-2722. All the supplies you need for ceramics, including kilns, glazes, greenware, and molds, can be found here. The Monroe Clayworks offers classes in a wide range of ceramic techniques. Class size is limited, so give them a call to see what's available, or just stop in.

Pookie's Fabrics: 615 Pawling Avenue, Troy, 272-6479. Over 5,000 bolts of fabric, quilting and sewing notions, patterns, books, etc. Get ready to sew!

Quiltbug: 3637 Carman Road, Schenectady, 280-2586. Quilters' fabric, notions, patterns, classes. You can order from their online store and never have to leave your house.

Stampassion Ltd.: 595 New Loudon Road, Newton Plaza, Latham, 782-7227. Stampassion stocks tons of rubber stamps and all the supplies you need to go with them. We are slightly addicted to these for illustrating our letters. (Wonderful, old-fashioned snail mail). Makes them more fun to read as well.

Nurseries and Greenhouses

Capital District Cooperative, Inc.: 381 Broadway, Menands, 465-1023. Drive around back behind the hardware store to find Esposito, Decker's Produce, and others offering bedding and other plants at wholesale prices. This is a great place to get the plants you need to start your garden.

Decker's Landscape and Aquatics: 1157 New Loudon Road, Latham, 608-5653; the big garden store is at 1632 Main Street, Pattersonville (west of Schenectady, before Amsterdam), 887-5552. We go to the Latham store for pond plants and supplies. If you blink, you'll drive right past it, so keep a look out once you pass Guptill's on Route 9. We bought a bunch of plants late in the season, and weren't expecting much, but everything survived a brutal winter and the lilies are flowering like mad. We have a tiny, hand-dug pond, but with the right plants it looks great. Decker's will be happy to help with your design.

Faddegon's Nursery, Inc.: 1140 Troy-Schenectady Road, Latham, 785-6726. The nursery features a large selection of all types of trees and shrubs, water plants, and garden décor, with a knowledgeable staff. They also can design your garden for you. We have had exceptionally good luck with everything we planted from here.

George's Market & Nursery: 240 Wade Road Extension, across from Target, Latham, 783-3474. George's continues to offer a huge selection of annuals, perennials, trees, shrubs, garden supplies, and gifts—all at great prices. Fresh produce in season, cider donuts, and fudge year round. The staff is very friendly and helpful.

Troy's Landscape Supply: 1266 New Loudon Road (Route 9), Cohoes, 785-1526. Offering a huge and unusual selection of plants, shrubs, and trees on 25 acres, Troy's Landscape also carries tools, rocks, and paving stones to help you design the perfect garden.

Valoze's Greenhouse: 5 Grove Lane (Route 9) Cohoes, 785-4343. Thousands of beautiful bedding plants are available in season.

Musical Instruments

A Violin Shop: 511 South Avenue, Schenectady, 370-0832. Lovely shop that sells, repairs, and restores violins.

Cole's Woodwind Shop: 47 Phila Street, Saratoga, 450-0333. Normally we wouldn't send you this far out of town, but Bill Cole has saved more than one of our trumpets from becoming a bugle. He specializes in high-end wind instruments. Has some beautiful vintage ones as well, and expert service for all of them.

Drome Sound: 3905 State Street, Schenectady, 370-3701. This store has been around for a long time, and we're always amazed that they can find the missing pieces to one of our musical instruments in one of their "boxes-o-stuff." Friendly and knowledgeable musicians work here.

Guitar Center: 145 Wolf Road, Albany, 446-1500. The big-box store of pop music instruments, Guitar Center offers a great selection and great prices. You can check all of the prices online before you get there.

Hermie's Music Store: 163 Jay Street, Schenectady, 374-7433. All kinds of instruments. They can repair that old clarinet you found in the attic, or build you the drum kit of your dreams.

John Keal Music Co.: 819 Livingston Street, Albany, 482-4405. Band instruments can be purchased or rented here; band equipment and sheet music is for sale.

Hilton Music Center: Colonie Center (lower level), Wolf Road, Albany, 459-9400. Drums, guitars, keyboards, amps. Plus accessories. They offer repairs as well. Good place for lessons.

Northeast Music: 885 New Loudon Road, Latham, 783-1658. Northeast provides quality concert band instruments to buy or rent, accessories, and repair.

Parkway Music: 1602 Route 9, Clifton Park, 383-0300. Chock-full of new and used instruments, amplifiers, and vintage items, this is a fun place to shop. They can fix any musical equipment and any kind of stringed instrument.

Segel Violins & Music Store: 44 3rd Street, Troy, 266-9732. Segal Violins specializes in high-quality instruments and sheet music, as well as expert repairs.

Schenectady Van Curler Music: 432 State Street, Schenectady, 374-5318. Mountains of sheet music and more from their online store (www.svcmusic.com/). Vintage, too! This is your source for NYSSMA sheet music. If you don't know what NYSSMA (New York State School Music Association) is, you don't belong here.

Used Vinyl and CDs

The Beat Shop: 197 River Street, Troy, 272-0433. Specializing in new and used, local and obscure music, the shop features frequent live performances, vinyl LPs, CDs, movies, and posters.

Blue Note Record Shop: 156 Central Avenue, Albany, 462-0221. Blue Note has been around for more than 65 years and carries a phenomenal collection of vinyl LPs and 45s, and a great jazz collection. Knowledgeable staff, as you would expect.

Last Vestige: 173 Quail Street, Albany, 432-7736. Thousands of records in every genre are in stock. Fun, fun, fun place to find things you must have.

Jewelry and Gifts

Artcentric: 266 River Street, Troy, 691-0007. Fun place to shop. Unusual gifts, antiques, and furnishings. Troy stuff. Packed.

Albany Institute of History and Art Gift Shop: 125 Washington Avenue, Albany, 463-4478. Most people don't think of the Institute as a shopping destination, but it houses a large and interesting gift shop stocked with jewelry, books, art, collectibles, and a whole lot more. It is easy to find a great gift here.

Annick Designs: 269 River Street, Troy, 273-7860. Beautiful, unique jewelry along with some amazing mineral specimens.

Blue Bird Home Décor: 11 3rd Street, Troy, 365-2138. This amazing store is so full of everything from vintage furniture, glorious paintings, unusual home accents, and an abundance of wonderful gift items, that we just don't know where to categorize it. Just go. You will love shopping here.

The Broken Mold Studio: 284 River Street, Troy, 273-6041. A number of different artists have created the lovely selection of pottery found in this studio.

The Counties of Ireland: 77 Third Street, Troy, 687-0054. This store contains a beautiful collection of sweaters, scarves, jewelry, and accessories, as well as food specialties imported from Ireland.

Elissa Halloran Designs: 229 Lark Street, Albany, 432-7090. Not only can you find original jewelry by the owner, but a number of local artists are represented here. There's also a consignment clothing boutique in the store. One of the easiest places to find a great gift in Albany.

Fort Orange General Store: 296 Delaware Avenue, Albany, 729-3703. Cool selection of handmade home goods and gifts, cute cards, and a neat bunch of Albany souvenirs.

Frank Adams Jewelers: 1475 Western Avenue (Stuyvesant Plaza), Albany, 435-0075. This is a family-run, very fine jewelry store where you can certainly find the perfect gift.

Hippies, Witches & Gypsies: 212 River Street, Troy, 326-1048. They call themselves an "eclectic shoppe" and they are, with candles, jewelry, minerals, potions, and clothing. Your place for the mystical side of you.

JK Bloom Jewelers: 21 3rd Street, Troy, 272-1807. Diamond jewelry, including engagement rings, are made right in the store. The designers can create just the ring you were hoping for. They can also repair your family heirlooms.

Maggie's Gift Shop: 521 Troy-Schenectady Road, Latham, 785-2629. Along with a tremendous selection of Alex and Ani bracelets, they carry all sorts of other collectibles, including Boyd's Bears, Lladro, Thomas Kinkade, Precious Moments, etc. Hard not to find a good gift here.

Mayfair Jewelers: 549 Troy-Schenectady Road (next to Starbucks), Latham, 785-7898. Mayfair carries a full selection of gold, diamonds, watches, and flatware. They also have done some really good repair work for us on some old pieces.

miSci Museum Gift Shop: 15 Nott Terrace Heights, 382-7890, in the museum. Most people overlook museum gift stores, but this is one of the best, with art and designer crafts, among other really cute science-museum merchandise.

Northeastern Fine Jewelry: 1575 Western Avenue, Albany, 862-9441; 1607 Union Street, Schenectady, 372-3604. Offering their customers beautiful jewelry and watches at great prices. They can custom design your dream ring or any other piece you want. They just want you to be happy. Just looking makes us happy.

Philip Alexander Jewelers: 471 Albany Shaker Road, Loudonville, 438-4810. This store has beautiful estate jewelry—lots of it—and gives appraisals. They buy, sell, and do expert repairs. Summer hours are very loose so call ahead of a visit.

Prism Glassworks: 225 4th Street, Troy, 273-4527. Brightly colored, funky, hand-blown glass pipes, goblets, jewelry, and marbles can be purchased here. They give lessons, too.

River Rocks Bead Shop: 209 River Street, Troy, 273-4532. River Rocks offers a huge selection of beautiful glass, silver, and gemstone beads with all the supplies you need to put them together. The shop sells one-of-a-kind designer jewelry and some gift items from around the world. They are closed Mondays.

Romanation Jewelers: 48 3rd Street, Troy, 272-0643. Romanation offers a large selection of fine jewelry and watches, as well as a very good selection of antique and estate jewelry.

Romeo's: 299 Lark Street, Albany, 434-4014. Romeo's carries a bunch of very cool everything, including vintage clothing, home décor, jewelry, cards, gifts, a full line of massage oils, and more.

Science and Hobby: 1632 2nd Avenue, Watervliet, 272-9040. This is an extensive hobby store that is stocked with everything from balsa wood to telescopes and RC cars. The most impressive part of the store is the huge RC racetrack with ramps and jumps. RC and nitro car enthusiasts gather on Sundays from October to March to race and show off. "Commentators" are welcome.

T&J Handcrafted Soap: 271 River Street, Troy, 272-2660. Lovely soaps and adorable soap accessories like towels and soap dishes.

Troy Cloth & Paper: 291 River Street, Troy, 687-1010. Original designs printed on clothing, cards, posters, notebooks, etc. Recycled paper, really fun.

Tough Traveler: 1012 State Street, Schenectady, 468-6844. Tough Traveler has been making its quality luggage, backpacks, kid and dog carriers, and other gear in the area since 1970. When you buy from them, you are getting quality while supporting the local economy at the same time.

Vince Kendrick Jewelers: 75 Remsen Street, Cohoes, 285-0998. Around for decades, this is one of the best stores for exquisite antique jewelry and new pieces. It's located in the former Cohoes Savings Bank—an art deco beauty that features seven of those huge murals by David Lithgow, and other deco design treats that make a visit here well worth the trip.

Wit's End Giftique: 1762 US Route 9, Clifton Park, 371-9273. OK so not really in town, but when you are desperate to find the right gift, they will have it here. They have everything: jewelry, clothing, shoes, bags, collectibles, gifts from around the world, and more.

Galleries (You Can Look at and Buy From)

Albany Center Gallery: 39 Columbia Street, Albany, 462-4775. With a rich 35-plus-year history, the gallery offers a great place to see some of the outstanding, creative work by local artists. If you live within a 100-mile radius and are a working artist, they may be looking for you.

The Arts Center of the Capital Region: 265 River Street, Troy, 273-0552. In the last few years, this arts center has really begun to shine. The shows are well curated and worth spending some real time looking at. The center offers dozens of classes and holds performances in the Joseph L. Bruno Theater. Start enjoying it at Troy Night Out.

Clement Frame Shop & Art Gallery: 201 Broadway, Troy, 272-6811. This gallery features changing monthly exhibits that focus on local artists, as well as a large selection of matted art and expert framing.

Fulton Street Gallery: 408 Fulton Street, Troy, 331-0217. Run solely by volunteers, this gallery focuses on local artists. If you are interested in becoming a member, give them a call. This place is really one of Troy's gems.

Martinez Gallery: 3 Broadway (upstairs), Troy, 274-9377. This is another of the galleries in Troy that we like a lot. The gallery focuses mostly on Latino and Latin American art, and every show is exciting.

PhotoCenter—The Photography Center of the Capital District: 404 River Street, Troy, 273-0100. As well as offering gallery space to its members, PhotoCenter has studio space and equipment for use by its members to pursue all aspects of photography. Basic membership begins at $35 per year (www.photocentertroy.org).

Upstate Artists Guild (UAG): 247 Lark Street, Albany, 694-3090. Exhibiting the art of more than 250 artists and administering Albany's First Fridays, UAG brings art to the masses. The guild hosts monthly gallery exhibitions as well as different workshops. You can and should become a member and support the arts in Albany.

Miscellany

In no particular order (except alphabetical):

Albany Barn: 46–48 North Swan Street, Albany, 56 Second Street, Albany, 935-4858. The old St. Joseph's Academy has been turned into an artists' building with affordable living and workspace. This is a creative-arts incubator, and includes all arts. They have a number of fund-raisers during the year, which help move this incredible idea forward.

Albany Theatre Supply: 445 North Pearl Street, Albany, 465-8895. Exactly. Need blackout cloth? It's here.

Bob's Trees: 1227 West Galway Road, Hagaman 882-9455. If you want to cut your own "holiday" tree, you can do it here, or just pick up a fresh-cut one. All kinds of trees can be found here. Great smells with a nice place to warm up with a cup of hot cocoa. Bob's may be far, but it's definitely worth the trip.

Captain JP Cruise Line: 278 River Street, Troy, 270-1901. During the warmer months, the Captain runs dinner cruises up and down the

Hudson. Call for the summer schedule or visit www.captainjp.homestead.com.

The Costumer: 1995 Central Avenue, Albany, 464-9031; and their original store at 1020–1030 Barrett Street, Schenectady, 374-7442. Costumes for purchase or for rent; this is a fun place to buy a gift for that hard-to-shop-for person.

Franklin Plaza: 4th and Grand streets, Troy, 270-9622. Planning a grand party or your dream wedding and have no idea where to hold it? Franklin Plaza just might be your answer. Located in an old banking building (the cloak room is the old vault), this establishment has a comfortable elegance and serves fabulous food. The building dates back to 1833 but was completely restored in 1992. The ballrooms are gorgeous, and the staff is very friendly and accommodating.

The Gas Menagerie: 1627 5th Avenue, Troy, 272-3087. Got a Jag or Range Rover that needs to be repaired? Patrick O'Reilly runs this one-man show from his small garage in Troy, and with 30-plus years' experience, he's one of the few who knows what he's doing and can expertly fix up your baby.

Gurley Precision Instruments: 514 Fulton Street, Troy, 272-6300. In the Gurley Building since 1862. Makers of optical encoders, optical coatings, and open-channel flow meters to measure water velocity—in case you ever find yourself needing these.

Historic Albany Foundation's Architectural Parts Warehouse: 89 Lexington Avenue, Albany, 465-2987. Missing doors, windows, plumbing parts, mantles, etc., for your old house? You might be able to find them here. Donations of historic house parts in good shape are accepted as well.

Infamous Signs & Graphics: 1706 Central Avenue, Albany, 459-7446. Full graphic and web design services are offered, and if you want to turn your car into a rolling billboard, these guys can give it a full-color vehicle wrap.

Lexington Vacuum: 997 Central Avenue, Albany, 482-4427. When you need the odd belt, hose, or bag, this is the place to go. They also sell vacuums and do repairs.

Orion Boutique: 169 Jay Street, Schenectady, 346-4902. This is the place for anyone who smokes, with offerings of tobacco, cigars, and pipes.

Powdertech Custom Powdercoated Finishes: 4779 Duanesburg Road, Duanesburg, 356-7431. Got any old, rusty lawn furniture? Or maybe a small airplane? They can make anything of any size look new again. And they're nice people too!

Screen-It Ltd.: 362 Congress Street, Troy, 272-1606. Whether it's your artwork or theirs, the service is always professional, fast, and friendly.

The Troy Book Makers: 291 River Street #180, Troy, 689-1083. No one willing to publish your book? Publish it yourself. They will guide you through the process and feature your book in one of their local bookstores. Helpful and knowledgeable.

The Water Garden Co. (part of Eddie's Aquarium): 898 New Loudon Road (Route 9), Latham, 783-3474. Do you want a peaceful pond in your backyard, but are just too lazy to do all the work to get it? These guys will do it for you, or fix the one you have and make it a working mini-ecosystem.

Event Calendar

Good Things Year Round

January

Albany Chefs' Food & Wine Festival—Wine & Dine for the Arts: A three-day festival in downtown Albany. Check www.albanywinefest.com for exact dates and times.

Friday Art Nights: It's cold. You could just stay inside; however, the Friday art nights go on all year. Albany: first Friday of the month; Troy: last Friday of the month; Schenectady: third Friday of the month.

Winter Festival and Ice Fishing Contest: Grafton Lakes State Park (www.friendsofgraftonlakes.org).

February

Dance Flurry in Saratoga Springs: Dance your way across the town (www.danceflurry.org).

Mac-n-Cheese Bowl: A one-day event to benefit the Regional Food Bank of Northeastern New York, most recently held at Siena College. Check timesunion.com/TableHoppingMac-n-CheeseBowl. Tickets available at Price Chopper.

New York in Bloom at the State Museum: A true breath of fresh air in winter (www.nysm.nysed.gov).

Schenectady County Winter Carnival: Maple Ski Ridge (www. schenectadycounty.com).

Times Union Home Expo: Times Union Center, timesunion homeexpo.com. One of the largest and longest-running home shows around.

March

St. Patrick's Day Parade: Downtown Albany. No explanation needed; wear your green and get cheap ice cream at Stewart's.

April

Star Parties: They begin this month at the Landis Arboretum. Sponsored by the Albany Area Amateur Astronomers; call 875-6935.

Tulips: Sit back and watch them grow.

May

Guptill's Flea Market (actually, this is the St. Nicholas Russian Orthodox Church's flea market next to Guptill's on Route 9 in Latham): Two times a year: one the Saturday before Mother's Day, and one mid-September. Over 200 vendors. Lots of everything and Russian/Polish food.

St. Sophia Greek Festival: St. Sophia Greek Orthodox Church, 440 Whitehall Road, Albany. Greek food, pastries, music, dance, rides, jewelry, souvenirs, and more!!!

Tulip Festival: Washington Park, Albany. Held on Mother's Day weekend, the festival is glorious in every way.

June

Alive at 5: Also starts this month in Albany, every Thursday at 5, at Corning Riverfront Park (in 2016, the concerts were held in Tricentennial Park due to construction so check the *TU Preview* section to be sure). Goes into August.

Art on Lark: Lark Street, Albany. This is a friendly street fair with lots of good local art and crafts. Check www.albany.org for specifics.

Capital Pride Parade: Washington Park and surrounding streets. Check www.albanyevents.org for date and time.

Flag Day Parade in Troy: Marching along Fourth Street, this parade is the biggest anywhere. Visit www.troyny.gov for date.

The Gas Up: Taking place on the second and third weekends of June, the Gas Up features antique engines doing all sorts of things, old-time steam shovels, old farm machinery, all running in a field in Schoharie. Visit http://www.thegasup.org/index.html for more info.

Music Haven Concert Series: Sundays in Schenectady's Central Park, starting this month and going into August.

Juneteenth: in Washington Park, a festival commemorating African American emancipation. Check www.albanyevents.org for date and time.

Rockin' on the River: Troy's Riverfront Park, music every Wednesday at 5 p.m.; starts in June and goes into August.

Troy River Fest: The festival features art and music in downtown Troy.

July

Free music in Albany: Corning Riverfront Park (Tricentennial Park in 2016). Alive at 5 continues on Thursdays. Fun, fun, fun.

July 4th Fireworks: All over the area on different dates, but the big show is at Empire State Plaza on the 4th. Check www.albany.com for a more complete list.

Park Playhouse: The playhouse starts its run of musical theater at the Lakehouse in Washington Park. These are professional-quality productions and they are *free*!! (www.parkplayhouse.com).

Saratoga Race Course: The racetrack opens for the season toward the end of July.

Troy's "Pig Out": This BBQ competition continues to be popular, so we imagine it will just keep getting bigger and better. This competition rounds up some of the best BBQ teams from the area and features music, crafts, and *fabulous* food.

A number of craft and other festivals are held in July, so check www.albany.org, or the *Times Union Preview* section on Thursday, for a complete listing.

August

Civil War Heritage Days: Schuyler Flatts Park, Route 32, Menands. This happens every August here. It is run by volunteers, and attended by a number of Civil War Camps, but there is no set website or person in charge. They've added a timeline of other historic events to the weekend, but there are always Civil War battle reenactments on both Saturday and Sunday. Start Googling "Civil War Heritage Days, Schuyler Flatts" in July and you can find dates and times.

Enchanted City: Troy hosts this steampunk themed festival. Art, performances, parade and amazing costumes. Chamberlain's Inventors' Challenge invites you to create a "mad mechanical conveyance." These have been especially intriguing the last couple of years. Please note that their date is never set in stone. 2016's event was in August but in 2015 it was in October. Best to check their website. theenchantedcitytroy.com

New York State Food Festival: Empire State Plaza. Food and Music. That's all you need. Check www.albanyevents.org.

Or, go to any number of fairs including:

The Altamont Fair

The Washington County Fair

Schoharie County Sunshine Fair

September

Albany Jazz Festival: Washington Park. Nonstop jazz from 1 to 9 p.m.

Capital District Scottish Games: Altamont Fairgrounds. The beginning of September (Labor Day weekend) brings us the Scottish Games. Men in kilts throwing logs—need we say more?

Capital Region Apple & Wine Festival: Altamont Fairgrounds. Usually held the second weekend after Labor Day. More than 100 crafters, wine and wine tasting of dozens of regional wines, and your favorite apples from Altamont Orchards!

Guptill's Flea Market: Route 9 next to Guptill's Arena. Usually the third Saturday of the month.

Irish2000Fest: Saratoga County Fairgrounds. This is a two-day festival with nonstop music (www.irish2000fest.com).

Larkfest: This is Lark Street's end-of-summer extravaganza with food, music, crafts, and *fun* (www.larkstreet.org).

Pearlpalooza: Music festival on Albany's Pearl Street sponsored by those wonderful people at WEQX.

Stockade Villagers Art Show: Schenectady's Historic Stockade District. This art show usually is held the weekend after Labor Day, but check the newspaper for the exact date.

Stockade Walkabout: Also this month; check it out at historicstockade. com.

Uncle Sam Parade in Troy: Visit www.troyny.gov for date and location.

Waterford Tugboat Roundup: Waterford. The roundup is usually the weekend after Labor Day, but make sure to double-check. More than two dozen old-time tugboats are open for touring, and there's music, food, fun kids' stuff, and fireworks (www.tugboatroundup.com).

Also in September:

Columbia County Fair, Fonda Fair, Schaghticoke Fair

October

Chowderfest: throughout downtown Troy, mid-October; check the Troy BID's website for times and location.

Goold Orchards Apple Fest: Goold hosts its annual Apple Fest on Columbus Day weekend with music, crafts, local wine, and of course delicious apples.

Haunted Halloween tours of the local mansions: Check www. albanyevents.org for dates and times.

Shaker Christmas Craft Fair: 1848 Shaker Meeting House, Shaker Heritage Society, Colonie. Held in the meeting house, this craft fair takes place from the end of October through Christmas week for stress-free shopping.

November

Capital Holiday Lights in the Park: Washington Park, Albany. The lights shine until January.

Capital Region Holiday Parade: State Street, Schenectady. This is the largest nighttime parade in the Northeast. Our very own Santa Claus parade.

December

Albany Last Run 5K: Sponsored by the City of Albany Office of Special Events, this evening race takes place mid-to-late December and runs you through the Capital Holiday Lights in the Park.

Annual Holiday House Tour in Albany: Sponsored by Historic Albany Foundation, the tour gives you the opportunity to peek inside a dozen of Albany's historic homes decked out for the holidays (www.historic-albany.org).

First Night: On December 31, Saratoga hosts a wonderful First Night throughout its beautiful downtown.

Santa Speedo Sprint: The sprint runs down Lark Street in Albany. Sponsored by the Albany Society for the Advancement of Philanthropy (ASAP), the sprint supports local charities (www.albanysociety.org).

Troy Victorian Stroll: Get dressed up like your great-great grandma (or grandpa) and head to downtown Troy for some music and entertainment. Enjoy shopping, eating, the lights, and more.

All Year Long

Remember!!!

Albany's First Friday: www.1stfridayalbany.org.

Schenectady's Art Night: Schenectady's Art Night is held the third Friday of each month (www.artnightschenectady.org).

Troy Night Out: This event is held the last Friday of each month (www.troynightout.org).

Schenectady Greenmarket: A year-round farmer's market right in downtown offering a wide and delicious selection of fresh produce, cheese, meats, milk, baked goods, etc. During the summer the market is located at City Hall, 105 Jay Street; in the winter it moves inside Proctors. It is open Sundays from 10 a.m. to 2 p.m. (374-1956).

Troy Waterfront Farmer's Market: Bringing you fresh produce, milk, cheese, meats, and so much more, the market is located inside the Uncle Sam Atrium on Broadway at 3rd and 4th streets in Troy every Saturday through April from 9 a.m. to 2 p.m. It moves outside to Troy's River Street in the spring, Saturday 9 a.m. to 2 p.m. (312-5749).

We're going to sneak one more recipe in here because it is a favorite with our friends and family, and it's a cinch.

Forgotten Cookies

Preheat oven to 400 degrees

3 egg whites
1 cup sugar
6 ounces (or a little more) chocolate chips
1 cup chopped pecans (you can just leave these out if you have nut
   allergy concerns)

Whip egg whites until very stiff, and gradually add sugar while continuing
to mix. Fold in chocolate chips (and nuts). Grease at least 3 cookie sheets,
and using two teaspoons, (one to spoon up and one to push onto the
sheet), place spoonfuls about 3/4-inch apart. Put trays in oven all at once,
and *turn off the oven and forget them* for at least 4 hours or overnight.
Makes dozens and dozens.

More Historical/Hysterical Events

Including Albany, Troy, and Schenectady:

March 1647: Fort Orange was nearly swept away by an unusually big flood that widened and deepened the river so much that a school of whales swam up the Hudson as far as Lansingburgh. One became stranded on an island opposite Lansingburgh, which became known as Whale Island. This island vanished during construction of the state dam.

August 15, 1649: The Patroon's brewery turns out 330 "tuns" (252 gal./tun) of beer during the year.

April 23, 1655: Speaking of beer, the Dutch East India Company decides to charge every home brewer a four-guilder tax on every tun they brew.

December 1658: 37,640 Beaver skins were shipped out of Fort Orange.

November 1663: A smallpox outbreak in Fort Orange took more than one life per day and as many as 1,000 Native American lives.

1664: King Charles figures out that there's money to be made in the Hudson Valley, so he gives the land to his brother with enough warships and men to steal it from the Dutch.

February 1666: Daniel De Remy de Courcelles led an army of 300 French militia down from Canada to fight the Dutch for their territory. On finding out that it was now no longer in Dutch hands but rather British, he said, "Excusez-moi," and returned without delay to Canada. He was provided with some provisions and wine for his troubles.

1681: Albanians are terrified by Newton's comet and write to the acting governor to see what they should do to escape God's wrath. It is decided that they should humble themselves and pray to God to withdraw his righteous judgment from them. (It is agreed, provided that they have to do this only once a month).

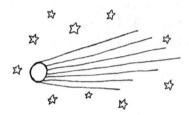

January 1687: John Caspers commits the first recorded murder in the city of Albany.

1689: With the impending French and Indian War, Mayor Pieter Schuyler felt that letting the people know about it "wolde make them run all madd." And so . . .

February 8, 1690: The Schenectady Massacre occurred. Indian and French entered the stockade and burned all but two houses and killed 60 men, women, and children. The locals were not expecting any French or Indian visitors and left the gates open and unguarded.

1695: Robert Livingston, while on a trip to England, meets Captain William Kidd, and they enter into a project that would allow qualified seamen to capture pirate ships. The English government agrees with Livingston's "skillfully conceived plan," which would allow those making the capture be allowed to keep the booty.

1696: Pirates infest the Hudson River, and Livingston and Governor Bellomont invest in a speedy boat to chase pirates, which they give to Captain William Kidd to command.

1698: Captain Kidd, being unsuccessful at capturing pirates, becomes one, using the speedy boat he was given. He becomes notorious as a terror of the seas.

November 23, 1697: John Ratcliffe is named the city porter of Albany. His job is to close the gates (now that we knew that that was a good idea) and to ring the bells at proper intervals.

July 26, 1700: According to a letter from Governor Coote, witchcraft was introduced into Albany from Canada. Too bad they didn't bring their evil universal health care. Those Canadians are so mean.

March 19, 1785: The Albany Common Council decides to ditch any seemingly English Street names and appoints a committee to come up with some new names and numbers.

June 1785: City officials authorize the demolition of Fort Frederick. Really trying to get rid of that whole England thing.

January 1787: The weight of a loaf of bread is fixed at 1 pound 12 ounces, for 4 coppers.

September 11, 1790: Albany Street names are officially changed. Goodbye to Howe, Prince, Gage Monckton, Wolfe, Hawke, Duke, and King. We really kept Wolf and Hawk, just got rid of that pesky British *e*.

April 10, 1792: Greenbush becomes a town, leaving behind its original name: Tuscameatic-Aet.

September 23, 1793: Fearful that Colonel Alexander Hamilton and his wife, Elizabeth Schuyler, were carrying yellow fever with them from Philadelphia, Albany had a team of physicians greet them at the Schuyler mansion and determine that they were pestilence free.

January 1796: *Morse's American Geography* of 1796 declares Albany's water to be "extremely bad, scarcely drinkable."

February 12, 1809: "Thermometer 12 below zero on west side of Pearl Street." No mention of the east side.

June 1810: Pierre Briare, "late Pastry Cook to one of the Princes of the Royal Family of Bourbons and to the Viceroy of Mexico," opens a place at No. 10 Green Street. La Serre sits pretty much on top of where this was.

February 1, 1819: A loaf of bread is now required by law to weigh 2 pounds 8 ounces.

June 3, 1828: De Witt Clinton's property was sold at auction to satisfy a judgement of $6,000. Nothing was left of the fine estate he once owned, and the man who fought for and implemented the Erie Canal died poor. The mammoth silver vases presented to him in recognition of the completion of the Erie Canal were sold for $600. They were valued at $3,500 at the time. In 1906 they were moved to the Metropolitan Museum of Art in New York.

May 5, 1824: The Albany Institute is formed by combining the Society for the Promotion of Useful Arts with the Albany Lyceum of Natural History. Useful arts here refer to agriculture and livestock management, with a little meteorology thrown in.

July 29, 1830: Gen. Stephen Van Rensselaer breaks ground for the first steam-operated railroad in Schenectady, to be called the Mohawk and Hudson. In 1847 the name changed to Albany and Schenectady Railroad, but this was absorbed by the New York Central Railroad in 1853. The Mohawk Hudson route is still maintained by, and is the oldest section of rails operated by, the CSX system.

1832: Cholera outbreak affects 387 citizens and kills 136 during the month of July. Everyone is asked to burn tar to abate the spread of the plague. The city turns dark and the street and shops are empty. By the end of August, 401 are reported dead. The plague is declared over on September 15, 1832.

September 1842: Musical instruction comes to public schools for the first time under the direction of Professor Ferdinand I. Ilsley.

1849: Cholera is back. About 700 cases with around 300 deaths for July and August.

1853: No cholera this summer, but 28 people die from the heat during the week of August 13.

1854: Cholera is back again for its summer visit.

August 28, 1856: The Dudley Observatory was dedicated. Blandina Dudley donated funds totaling $62,000 to build the observatory in her husband's (Mayor Charles E. Dudley) memory. The hill it was built on (Arbor Hill) was donated by Stephen Van Rensselaer. The observatory burned down May 16, 1904. The organization lives on.

September 23, 1856: 100 people watching a burning canal boat from the State Street Bridge fall into the river.

April 27–28, 1860: Charles Nalle, a fugitive slave, was captured by US Marshals in Troy, but rescued by a visiting Harriet Tubman and the Vigilance Committee of Troy, only to be recaptured in Watervliet and again rescued the next day, by the same, where he was then whisked away and hidden in Niskayuna until his freedom could be bought. Nalle's owner happened to be his younger half brother. This was one of Troy's great moments, and is commemorated by a plaque at State and 1st.

1875: Population of Albany is 85,541. In 1892 it was 97,120. 1910—100,253. 1930—127,412. 1960—129,726. *Empire State Plaza Built*, 1970—110,000. 1980—101,727. At this writing it is 98,424.

May 8, 1878: Telephone exchange is established, with 100 members; the first ones to have a phone installed were seven local doctors. A few other phones were installed in public halls, shown as curiosities.

May 1878: Kenmore Hotel opens. The Kenmore was built by an African American named Adam Blake whose father was a slave belonging to Stephen Van Rensselaer. Legs Diamond used to party in its Rain-Bo Room. The Kenmore is still here at 74 North Pearl in Albany.

September 1882: It was reported that cricket was popular in Albany.

August 28, 1883: Beaver Creek is declared a public nuisance by the health board.

May 1, 1884: Albany Bicycle Club, which was organized in 1880, incorporates. They try to get bike lanes installed to no avail.

March 11, 1888: Commencement of the "terrible three-day blizzard."

August 30, 1888: Burns Statue is dedicated in Washington Park. The statue was a gift from Miss Mary McPherson.

November 17, 1891: *Times-Union* is first published.

September 29, 1893: The Moses statue is dedicated in Washington Park, a gift from Henry I. King in memory of his father.

April 1894: Mohawk and Hudson River Humane Society is incorporated, combining societies for the care of maltreated *children* and animals.

June 22, 1894: We will use the direct quote from the *Albany Chronicles* of 1906. "Paul Jones, globe-trotter, having started nude and penniless from Boston, visits Press Club."

August 15, 1900: Louis Menand, noted horticulturist and founder of Menands, died at his home there at 93. He was born in Burgundy, France.

April 26, 1905: Byron Travers, a guest at the Kenmore Hotel, was given the wrong satchel at checkout. This one contained $5,000 in diamonds. What a delightful parting gift.

December 26, 1905: It was rumored that Miss Elsie Smith, a former Queen Titania of the Halloween carnival, was sent poisoned candy!

Space—Because We Like It

Even in the city you can see some of the brightest stars and planets. We are regularly visited by spectacular meteor showers and an occasional comet, and the space station passes overhead at regular intervals. You can see a lot of this without a telescope (and they are mostly frustrating for we amateurs), but a good pair of astronomical binoculars will not only get you closer to a wider swath of the sky, but also to the comings and goings of your neighbors. (No, you really shouldn't spy on them.) This is the basic guide, so you'll know what to look for, and what you're looking at.

The Sun

The Sun is the star in the center of the Solar System. It is not the biggest or the hottest star in the universe, but it seems to work perfectly for us. The Sun is a giant ball of gas (72 percent hydrogen, 26 percent helium, and 2 percent heavier stuff like nitrogen, oxygen, and carbon). We get heat and light from the Sun due to nuclear fusion. When random nuclei of hydrogen bump into each other and merge, helium is produced and a whole lot of energy is released. The Sun has been doing this for about 4.5 billion years and is expected to keep right on doing this for another 4.5 billion years. It has a diameter of 864,000 miles, dwarfing anything else in the Solar System. Although it is about 400 times the size of the moon, it is also about 400 times as far away, so to us here on Earth, the Sun and moon look to be about the same size. The Sun does not have a formal name like other stars in the sky. It was called Sol, the sun god, and the Solar System is named for it.

Constellations You Should Know

There are 88 constellations in the sky, and up here in the Northern Hemisphere, we get to see half of them. As the Earth is making its way around the Sun, you get to look at different constellations. Most are seasonal and are in the sky for 10 months out of the year, vacationing behind the Sun for the other two. The ones we call the winter constellations are the ones that are out when we want to look at them in the winter, generally between 8 and 11 p.m.; the summer constellations are out between 9 p.m. and 1 a.m. Some are near the North Star, stay with us year round, and are called circumpolar constellations. To know what you're looking for, get your hands on *The Stars: A New Way to See Them* by H. A. Rey of "Curious George" fame. It was written in 1952 and has been continually updated. It's still one of the best books on the stars around for any age. Winter has our favorite stars because they are so easy to recognize. Facing south toward the west, Orion shines brightly with his three-star belt and four bright stars marking his arms and legs. The star to the top left is a red star named Betelgeuse, which translates to "armpit of a giant." Going west, you will see the V-shaped head of Taurus the Bull with the asterism, the Pleiades (seven sisters) riding on his shoulder. Left of and lower than Orion is the brightest star in the Northern Hemisphere, Sirius, which is one of the stars in the Canis Major (great dog) constellation. Above this is a sort of rectangular shape, which outlines the Gemini Twins. To their left (east) is Leo the Lion. He looks like a backward question mark. Turn around, and facing north, to your left (west) you should see the big W, Cassiopeia, the vain queen, and then going toward the east, you should see the Little Dipper or Bear—Ursa Minor, then Draco the Dragon, and then toward the right, the Big Dipper, which is not a constellation, but an asterism, which lives inside the Big Bear or Ursa Major. Can't find the Little Dipper? Use the two stars on the outside edge of the Big Dipper's bowl, connect the dots, and it will point you to the North Star, which is the tip of the tail of the Little Dipper. In the summer, wait until after 9:30 and then look up and see if you can find a bright star. It should be overhead. This is Vega, part of the constellation Lyra the Harp. Facing east, to the left of Vega will be the Northern Cross or Cygnus the Swan. To the right is another pretty bright star, which is Altair, part of Aquila the eagle. Just below these three constellations will be Delphinus, the dolphin. If you find yourself with an open view, look toward the south, your right, and find Scorpius hugging the horizon. He has a red star at his heart called Antares. The north will still have the circumpolar stars of the Dippers, Draco, and Cassiopeia. It takes your eyes over two hours to get sensitive enough to see the stars, so plan on some time outside.

The Planets

There are eight planets in the Solar System: Mercury, Venus, Earth, Mars, Jupiter, Saturn, Uranus, and Neptune.

Mercury

Mercury is the small planet closest to the Sun. It was named for the Roman god Mercury, who was the winged messenger to the other gods (and he was very fast). Because Mercury could be seen moving around the Sun so quickly this seemed a very appropriate name. Thousands of years ago, the Greeks thought Mercury was actually two planets, one visible at dawn and the other at dusk. The morning planet was called Apollo and it wasn't until the fifth century BC that Pythagoras realized they were one and the same. About 30 years ago, the Mariner 10 Spacecraft came close to Mercury and gave us more information. Mercury is called an inferior planet because it is between Earth and the Sun. This also makes it hard for us to get a good look at it because it is usually lost in the glare of the Sun. It is visible only for up to two hours before dawn or after dusk, and only at certain times of the year. These times are when Mercury is at its greatest elongation—or when it appears to be furthest from the Sun from Earth's vantage point. Mercury is about 36 million miles from the Sun and only takes 88 days to go around it.

Venus

Venus is the second-closest planet to the Sun. It is named for the Roman goddess of love and beauty because of its brightness in the morning and evening skies. Like Mercury, Venus also was thought to be two planets, the morning star Eosphorus and the evening star Hesperus. (Astronomers knew it was just one planet early on.) Also, like Mercury, Venus is an inferior planet located between Earth and the Sun. The first spacecraft to visit this lovely planet was Mariner 2 in 1962. Because it has a thick cloud cover, information was gathered using infrared technology. It was once thought that Venus was Earth's twin, looking to be about the same size and makeup. However similar the planets might have been early in development, Venus is nothing like Earth and is probably the most inhospitable of all of the planets. The closeness to the Sun boiled away any liquid there might have been, and greenhouse gases sealed its fate. Venus's atmosphere holds in the heat of the Sun, making it hotter than Mercury. It is about 67 million miles from the Sun, and its "year" is 224.7 Earth days. Inferior planets never appear fully lit and appear to us in phases like the moon. Venus, being one of the brightest objects in the sky, has often been mistaken for a UFO because of this. A very bright, oddly shaped light in the sky must be a spaceship.

Earth

Earth! We live here, which is an amazing fact all by itself. Earth is located about 93 million miles from the Sun, which makes us neither too cold nor too hot. Somewhere in our distant past it is suggested that an asteroid hit the Earth, which gave us our water source. Seventy percent of the Earth's surface is covered in ocean, and 80 percent of all photosynthesis takes place in these oceans. Earth is the only planet in the Solar System that is not named after a Greek or Roman god but rather is named after what it is—earth or ground—from the Old English *oerthe*. Originally it was believed that Earth was the center of the Solar System, an idea pushed by Ptolemy in the second century. It wasn't until 1543 when Copernicus, a Polish astronomer, came up with the model placing the Sun in the center of the Solar System. Earth originally was thought to be flat, but it became apparent looking at the Earth's shadow crossing the moon during eclipses that it indeed was a round planet. The Earth has a wonderful 23-degree tilt that allows us to have seasons as we orbit around the Sun. At the center of the Earth is a core of nickel and iron. This, combined with its motion, creates a dynamo producing the magnetic field. The Earth's diameter is 7,926 miles, and its year lasts 365¼ days. We also have one beautiful moon.

Mars

Mars is the fourth planet from the Sun and the last of the terrestrial or rocky planets before we hit the asteroid belt. Like all of the other planets (except Earth), Mars gets its name from a Greek or Roman god. Ancient cultures associated the red color of this planet with blood and so named it after the Roman god of war, Mars. (The Greeks named their god of war Ares.) Although only about half the diameter of Earth, Mars is the most like Earth of all the planets. It has almost the same tilt, giving it very similar seasons; its day is only 30 minutes longer than ours. It is about 50 million miles farther from the Sun than the Earth, so every season is much colder and longer (its year is 687 days long). Mars has two smallish moons (most likely captured asteroids, rather than leftover planet material) named Phobos and Deimos (fear and panic—the Greek names for the dogs,or children, of Ares). Mars also is home to the highest known mountain in the Solar System—Olympus Mons—as well as the largest canyon. Mars has frozen polar icecaps that are easily seen with a telescope. Sadly, no Martians have been found by the rovers Spirit, Opportunity, or Curiosity, or by any of the orbiting satellites.

Jupiter

The first planet on the other side of the asteroid belt is the largest planet in the Solar System. Jupiter is named for the Roman king of the gods (the Greeks called theirs Zeus). In the night sky, Jupiter is brighter than most stars and is easily seen without a telescope. It is so big that it would take 1,000 Earths smooshed together to equal it. Unlike the four closest planets to the sun, which are rocky, solid spheres, Jupiter is an enormous ball of gas and liquid. Even though it is so large, it spins faster on its axis than any other planet, having a day that lasts only 9 hours and 56 minutes. The surface is marked with beautiful ribbons of different-colored clouds (all caused by different chemicals at different heights). The Great Red Spot of Jupiter is one of its most outstanding features. It is a reddish-brown, swirling storm that has been viewed for more than 400 years (basically since the telescope was invented). The spot itself has a diameter three times larger than Earth's. On its trip to Pluto, the New Horizons spacecraft found a smaller red spot, which was nicknamed Little Red. Jupiter has 62 moons, some having eruptions that shoot hundreds of miles into space. Jupiter also has three wispy little rings near its equator. Jupiter is 483 million miles from the Sun and takes 11.86 Earth years to orbit it.

Saturn

Saturn is the second largest planet in the Solar System and the sixth from the Sun. It also happens to be most people's favorite because of its beautiful rings. Saturn has thousands of rings, which were first observed by Galileo in 1610. Every 15 years, the Earth passes through the plane of Saturn and faces the rings edge on, which means, the rings seem to vanish. This happened in 2009, so we'll get to see the rings through 2024. Saturn's name is from the Roman god Saturnus—the same god as the Greek's Kronos or Cronus, the Titan god who ruled time and the ages. Kronus also is the god who ate all of his children, except Zeus.

Saturn's long and majestic trip around the sun (almost 30 years) was the inspiration for its name. Although its chemical makeup is much like that of Jupiter, its distance from the sun, at 886.7 million miles, makes it cooler, and the chemical reactions have less pizzazz. Saturn has more than 60 moons, 52 of which have formal names.

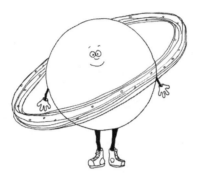

Uranus ('yūr-ə-nəs)

William Herschel discovered this planet in 1781 and named it the "Georgian Sidus" after King George III of England. The name Uranus came into use in 1850, when it was thought that we should keep the theme going and name it for one of the Greek or Roman deities. Uranus was the name of the Greek's earliest supreme god, son of Gaia and father of Cronus. Uranus is the seventh planet from the Sun and the third largest by diameter. It is considered an ice giant, composed mostly of rock and ice. Whereas Jupiter and Saturn are mostly hydrogen and helium, Uranus is only about 15 percent hydrogen. Looking through a telescope, you can see its beautiful blue-green color and its sideways rotation. Uranus has a diameter of 31,814 miles, about four times that of Earth. Uranus has 11 known rings and 21 named moons (and a handful of no-names). Most of its moons have Shakespearian names, which in a lot of cases are named after mythological characters, kind of like the planets. Uranus is 1.783 billion miles from the sun and takes 84.01 Earth years to orbit it.

Neptune

Once Uranus was found, it became apparent that there must be another planet out there, messing around with Uranus's orbit. So, the hunt was on for another planet. On September 23, 1846, Neptune was observed by Galle and d'Arrest at the Berlin observatory using French astronomer Le Verrier's calculations. Using calculations from English astronomer Adams, Challis, at the Cambridge Observatory, observed Neptune almost at the same time. Adams and Le Verrier were given equal credit. The name Neptune, for the Roman god of the sea, was suggested by Le Verrier, and recently, papers suggest that it was Le Verrier's work that really found the location of Neptune and that Adams was quite a bit off. Regardless, Galileo *really* saw it first in 1612. Neptune is the eighth and last real planet in the Solar System. It again is an ice giant, having a higher content of water, ammonia, and methane than either of the gas giants. It owes its deep blue color to trace levels of methane. Its diameter is 30,198 miles, just slightly smaller than Uranus. Neptune has faint rings like Uranus and 13 known moons. It is 2.793 billion miles from the Sun and takes 164.79 Earth years to orbit it.

Pluto, Dwarf Planets, and Plutoids

We like Pluto, so we are going to talk about it as though it is still a real planet. Pluto was discovered by chance by a 23-year-old Kansas astronomer named Clyde Tombaugh, who had just arrived at work at the Lowell Observatory in Arizona in 1930. He found it by comparing photographs to see if any objects seemed to change position in a 2-week period. Pluto did. Venetia Burney, an 11-year-old Oxford girl who was interested in mythology, named it Pluto, which is another name for Hades, the god of the underworld. Pluto was chosen not just because it was a cool name, but that the first two letters were the initials for Percival Lowell, whose observatory it was first seen from. The name became official on March 24, 1930.

Pluto is a very tiny planet, called a dwarf planet. It has a 1,429-mile diameter, or 18 percent of the Earth's. It also takes a very elliptical path around the Sun, a trip that takes 247.69 Earth years and passes inside Neptune's orbit for around 20 of those years. This last happened between 1979 and 1999—before that, about 150 years ago. Pluto has one very big moon named Charon, which it fights with for dominance in its orbit. It also has a couple of little tiny moons that we have only just recently found. The spaceship New Horizons successfully woke up after its nine-year journey and has been sending back all kinds of wonderful information about everyone's favorite dwarf planet. (Some of Clyde Tombaugh's ashes went along for the fly-by!)

When we started to discover more planet-like objects out there, the International Astronomical Union decided it was time to re-categorize things, and Pluto's place in the Solar System changed (figuratively). With the discovery of the small planet Eris in the Kuiper belt, and uncertainty over what to do about Ceres, the larger-than-Pluto asteroid, it was decided to make a new grouping called dwarf planets. So, in 2006, poor Pluto got demoted. Then, in 2008, the IAU decided to create another grouping called plutoids, basically any planet-like object past Neptune. So now, Pluto is not only a dwarf planet, but also a plutoid and a plutino—a whole other story. At this writing, we have one, "just a" dwarf planet, Ceres, and a number of dwarf-planet plutoids, which include Pluto, Eris, and Make Make. (Make Make was discovered during Easter time in 2005, so the name was taken from Easter Island meaning "the creator of humanity.")

Fun Things You Can Look for in the Sky!!

Meteor Showers!!!

Meteor showers occur when the Earth passes through a debris field left by a comet. They are named for the constellation that they seem to fall from, not for the comet they came from. We can see them following pretty regularly. And always on or within a day of these dates.

January 3–4, Quadrantids: There used to be a constellation named the Quadran Muralis in the northeastern sky, which is what these were named for. The constellation was eliminated from the lineup, but its stars are still there near Bootes and Ursa Major (the great bear—look for the big dipper).

April 21–22, Lyrids: Near Lyra the harp.

May 4–6, Eta Aquarids: Near Aquarius.

July 28–29, Delta Aquarids: Also near Aquarius.

August 12, Perseids: Near Perseus.

October 21, Orionids: Near Orion. Are we catching on yet?

November 16, Leonids: Near Leo.

December 13, Geminids: Near the Gemini twins.

Science 101

Northern lights. We don't see these very often, but when we do, they are very cool. But *why* do they occur? The Sun is where it all starts. The Sun is a big ball of gas that releases zillions of charged particles (ions) in its day-to-day activity of nuclear fusion. Sometimes the Sun gets really active and there are major flare-ups, which release even more of these ions and send them out into space (solar wind). Now they could just float around out there, but they are charged particles and they can be steered around by a magnetic field. Now, if you've ever played with a compass, you should know that the Earth has magnetic poles, so it's like a big magnet. As the solar wind reaches the Earth, its charged particles are steered to the North and South Poles by the magnetic field. The colors appear as the Sun's ions excite Earth's ions and make different molecules of different gases. Oxygen will emit a green color, nitrogen a blue one, and hydrogen a red one. At the North Pole we call the colorful display the northern lights or the Aurora Borealis. In the south you would see the southern lights or the Aurora Australis. If there is a chance of seeing northern lights, your local weatherman will usually give you a heads up.

Websites for You to Visit

www.skymaps.com: This will give you the monthly goings on of the stars and planets.

http://stardate.org/nightsky/: This is from the University of Texas's McDonald Observatory and is a great website containing tons of information.

http://www.seasky.org/: This is a website put up by an excellent amateur astronomer and sea lover named J. D. Knight. Again, lots of fun information here.

www.nasa.gov/: You could spend days here seeing what's up with the universe.

Some of Our Sources That We Are Willing to Reveal

A Godchild of Washington by Katharine Schuyler Baxter

Albany Architecture edited by Diana S. Waite

www.albanybarn.org

Albany Chronicles by Cuyler Reynolds

Albany.Com: http://www.albany.com

Albany Visitor's Center: www.albany.org

All Over Albany: http://alloveralbany.com

www.answers.com

Astronomy magazine

www.danceflurry.org

Encyclopedia Britannica: the real one that sits on a bookshelf

www.famousamericans.net

First Church: www.firstchurchinalbany.org/

www.1stfridayalbany.org

From Harlem to the Rhine by Major Arthur Little

Historic Albany Foundation

http://historicalmarkerproject.com

The Hudson Through the Years by Arthur G. Adams

In Order to Form a More Perfect Union by Samuel B. Fortenbaugh Jr.

In and Around the Capital Region by Ann Morrow and Anne Older

Keep Albany Boring: keepalbanyboring.com

www.larkstreet.org

Mayor Erastus Corning: Albany Icon, Albany Enigma by Paul Grondahl

The Mentor: The Story of the Hudson by Albert Bushnell Hart (August 1, 1917)

Memoirs of an American Lady by Anne Grant

Metroland "best of" guides: metroland.net. Special note here. After 38 years in the Capital Region, *Metroland* is no more. This was one of the best, truly Albany fixtures, that gave us an up-to-date weekly reading of everything that was going on—for free!!! Nothing else comes close. We remain blindly optimistic that someone with vision and $$ will step up and bring back this treasure. Or maybe just a thousand people with $100 each could do the same. Here's hoping.

http://nightsky.jpl.nasa.gov

www.nysm.nysed.gov/albany

www.nysparks.com/historic-sites

O Albany by William Kennedy

www.pbs.org

Philip Hooker by Edward W. Root

Rank and File by Theodore Roosevelt Jr.

Rensselaer County Historical Society: http://www.rchsonline.org

www.roadsideamerica.com/story/29462

Rosa Ponselle, A Singer's Life by Rosa Ponselle and James Drake

www.sayschenectady.org/

See Albany magazine

stleonardcommunity.blogspot.com (Kratina Uncle Sam Statue)

St. Mary's Church: www.hist-stmarys.org/

St. Peter's Church: stpeterschurchalbany.org

www.smithsonianmagazine.com

www.space.com

Studies for Albany by Arnold William Brunner & Charles Downing Lay

www.tenbroeckmansion.org

timesunion.com

www.troyny.gov

Uncle Sam: The Man and the Legend by Alton Ketchum

undergroundrailroadhistory.org/

Upper Hudson Valley Beer by Craig Gravina & Alan McLeod

www.volunteermatch.org

Voyage of the Paper Canoe by N.H. Bishop

Waterford Harbor Visitor Center

Wikipedia

See, we didn't make it all up!

Index

The Smalbanac can be reached at smalbanac@gmail.com or www.smalbanac.com.

Some people weren't quite sure who *this* was supposed to be. Since we use him all over the *Smalbanac*, we thought we'd let you know it's not Shakespeare. It's supposed to be Henry Hudson, hence the monogrammed HH on his shirt or cape. Hope this clears up the confusion.